MONEY&
POWER

The History of Business

Howard Means

with a Foreword by David Grubin

John Wiley & Sons, Inc.

New York • Chichester • Weinheim • Brisbane • Singapore • Toronto

ISBN 0-471-40053-X

Printed in the United States of America.
10   9   8   7   6   5   4   3   2   1

To George Watts Carr, Jr.

⚜ Contents ⚜

☙ Foreword ❧

by David Grubin

HEN BRUNO COHEN, CNBC'S SENIOR VICE PRESI-
dent, asked me if I would consider producing a
documentary about the history of business, I wondered aloud whether it would be possible. Where
does a story with such a vast scope begin, I asked him, and
where does it end? We'd like you to figure that out, Bruno said,
but he assured me that he and his boss, Bill Bolster—the man
behind CNBC's phenomenal success as a network devoted to
business news—were certain it could be done, and they wanted
me to give it a try. Two years later, the two-hour documentary
"Money and Power," produced by Ed Gray and Nick Davis
with the assistance of Amanda Pollak, Annie Wong, and Alex
Dionne, proved to me that they had been right.

This splendid book by Howard Means explores the same
themes as our film, but extends and elaborates upon them,
adding new material we didn't have the time or inclination to
include. I've always believed that a television documentary
should make you want to sit down and read a book. This companion volume to our program will allow you the pleasure of
doing just that.

I usually start work on a film ignorant and uncertain, and
this one was no exception, but there was one thing I was sure
of: I didn't want "Money and Power" to be an illustrated essay.
I could have begun, for example, with a pan across a herd of
brindled cows grazing on a mountainside meadow lit by the
early morning sun, the narrator explaining that cattle are one
of the oldest forms of wealth, and noting that our word *capital*

is derived from the Latin for a herd of cattle, *caput*. But as Casey said when he let the ball sail over the plate without taking a swing, "Ain't my style." I'm a storyteller. Rather than fashion an analytic economic history, I wanted to do what film does at its best: tell stories, not about history, but about people—who, after all, make history.

But what idea would bind the various stories together and make them relevant to our own time and place? When I considered how we go about our lives each day, the comforts we enjoy, the luxuries available, I found the connection to the past I was looking for. Today most of us who live in the Western world know an abundance beyond the wildest dreams of yesterday's richest king. We eat better, live longer, can travel farther and faster. We take our daily pleasures for granted, rarely pausing to consider that it hasn't always been this way. Viewed through the long lens of history, we in the West are a privileged few. Through the development of great industries and banks and of vast networks of mass communication and transportation, the West has become the center of the most productive economic engine the world has ever known.

How did it happen? That was a compelling question. To try and provide some answers I decided to tell the stories of people whose lives were emblematic of forces that were larger than themselves. The careers of the great tycoons—for example, the Rockefellers and the Morgans, the Medicis and the Rothschilds—were object lessons in the creation of private and public wealth. I would begin a thousand years ago, when the West was an economic backwater and nearly everyone lived by farming. Banking had not been invented, merchants were few, factories almost unknown. The Catholic Church, which defined the social, religious, and political climate of the times, no more encouraged trade than did the archaic numbering system, which made calculation difficult for anyone who needed to tally profit and loss. The price of goods was often set by custom, and trade was mostly a matter of barter and exchange, centering on small towns and manors. In the year 1000, the people of the Western world were no richer than those anywhere else on the planet. The Chinese and the Arabs were wealthier, more technologically advanced. No one then could have predicted that the West would one day outstrip every other culture in the accumulation of riches and power.

Scientists and politicians, artists and scholars, all contributed to the millennium of change, but the world's businessmen—its bankers, industrialists, merchants, and entrepreneurs—were a powerful driving force behind the stunning transformation. In telling their stories, I could explore a fundamental paradox: The great business moguls, sometimes ruthless, sometimes charitable, always bent on accumulating vast fortunes for themselves, helped create the modern world.

We decided to begin our film by standing viewers on their heads—shaking up their preconceptions by inviting them into a world with ideas and values radically opposed to their own. One thousand years ago, business as we know it did not exist. Life centered on the church, which discouraged innovation and change. The notion that the love of money is the root of all evil served as a warning that the life of the spirit was more important than getting rich, and the feudal system, with serfs working the land for lords of the manor, made it difficult for new wealth to be created that everyone could share. But in spite of limited economic opportunities, there was a growing demand for more exotic goods—tapestries, jewels, and spices— from noblemen and even members of the church itself. And there were already a few hardy merchants who were determined to pursue a more vigorous path with regard to their own purses.

Godric of Finchale was one of them. Forsaking the ties that bound him to the land, he accumulated a vast fortune trading on the high seas, then gave it all to the poor, retiring to a lonely forest in northern England where he dedicated the rest of his life to God. He came to be known as a holy man, and in the end was canonized by the church as a saint.

Godric was the first businessman we profiled in our film. It's interesting that he was vilified in his own time as a man of ruthless ambition, then became what we would call in our day a philanthropist. Whether he sought to assuage his guilt, improve his image, or simply to help those less fortunate than he was, it's hard to say now because facts are few and he lived when history easily blended into legend. But the similarity of his story to the Medicis, the Rockefellers, and Bill Gates is difficult to ignore—although none of these latter-day moguls are likely to ever be canonized.

Starting with Godric we would span 1,000 years, telling how the merchant Cosimo de' Medici became the greatest banker of his day, as powerful as the pope himself; how King Philip II of Spain squandered the gold that had made Spain the richest country on earth; how industrialist Matthew Boulton provided inventor James Watt with the secrets of finance and marketing that made Watt's steam engine the dynamo behind the Industrial Revolution. And we would go on to tell the stories of towering American businessmen and their creations: J.P. Morgan and his banking empire, John D. Rockefeller and Standard Oil, Henry Ford and the Model T, Henry Luce and *Time* magazine, Robert Woodruff and Coca-Cola, Harry and Jack Warner and Warner Bros., Bill Gates and Microsoft.

Along the way we would witness the creation of banking and the first stock exchange; the beginning of the industrial revolution and the building of the great railroads in America; the invention of the automobile; the birth of advertising, the movies, the computer, and the Internet. From a time when economies were local and money largely unknown, we would be catapulted into our own world—where money instantly leaps across borders electronically in a nonstop, 24-hour world economy.

I'm delighted that Howard Means has taken this story off the television screen and put it down on the page for you to consider at your leisure. Television brings the past alive like no other medium, but prose gives you the time to meditate upon it.

When I meditate on the formidable figures who people this story, I remember *Citizen Kane,* and the wealthy businessman who told an impecunious young reporter that "It's easy to make a lot of money if all you want to do is make a lot of money." I've never been sure whether the businessman was chiding himself or mocking the poor reporter because, after all, it's not easy to make a lot of money, but in any case, it is sometimes difficult to decide what you want, and that's something I like to think about.

INTRODUCTION

I N THE LONG SWEEP OF HISTORY, BUSINESS IS BOTH nearly as old as human beings and almost brand new. The Phoenicians were famous seagoing merchants. By 1500 B.C., the Chinese had established sophisticated markets in all manner of luxury goods, from silk to turquoise and tortoise shells. Money changers, the first bankers, are found in the Bible, doing the unglamorous but necessary work of stabilizing currencies across widely divergent cultures.

The Greeks, the Egyptians, and the Abyssinians all did business—they couldn't have avoided it even had they wanted to. We humans seem to have been programmed from the beginning to deal—to swap risk and reward in the pursuit of gain. If we could peer back far enough into the unrecorded history of the planet, we undoubtedly would find cave dwellers storing up sturdy clubs to trade for a mammoth flank or the skin of a saber-toothed tiger when the moment was right.

Business with a capital *B*, though—business not just as a way of providing but as a system of social and economic organization—emerges only within the last ten centuries, and for the most part far more recently than that.

Until people began to break free from the monarchies and theocracies that so limited and controlled their destinies, they had neither sufficient opportunity to pursue profit nor much incentive. Why strive so hard to make what you are so unlikely to be able to keep? Early businesspeople were also faced with reconciling their desire for a successful return on their investment—of time, labor, or money—with religious prohibitions against excessive gain: They had their souls to look to, the ultimate bottom line.

Labor markets and consumption markets had to be created. Means of production had to be improved. Capital mechanisms had to be established and refined. Transportation needed to be up to the challenge of moving goods and services to those places where they were most likely to reap the greatest rewards. People had to both broaden their horizons—I want that which I cannot see or procure on my own—and simultaneously narrow them: Exotic markets weren't impossibly far away; they were just far enough away to make it worthwhile to trade in what they had to offer. A human revolution, in short, had to take place before capital-*B* Business could set roots and grow. And grow. And grow.

That all this happened most dramatically in western Europe attests to a parallel political revolution as well. In part thanks to the Greeks and Romans, in part thanks to the independent spirit of the conquering hordes that ravaged Europe through much of the first millennium, the beginnings of democratic government, of self-determination, first seem to have set their hooks in the hearts of those who lived on the western extreme of the Eurasian land mass.

Runnymede and the Magna Carta ring out loud in the history of politics, but they ring out just as loud in the history of business. People had to be free before they could act freely.

They had to win the rights of self-governance and economic self-determination simultaneously. Being free to pursue political fortune almost inevitably entailed the freedom to pursue economic fortunes. The two cross-fertilized, and as they did, business began to blossom.

It was the two great and parallel revolutions of the last half of the last millennium that finally put business over the top. The Industrial Revolution created the means of mass production, just as the American Revolution was creating the world's first great experiment in democratic capitalism. The congruence between the two is almost spooky: James Watt first demonstrated his steam engine publicly on March 8, 1776, in Birmingham, England, less than four months before the American Founding Fathers met in Philadelphia to declare independence from Great Britain. Once again, politics and business were marching hand in hand, to the benefit of both. Soon the two would find themselves wedded to a companion Consumer Revolution: As more production capacity came on line, people gained more capacity to purchase, and as they gained more capacity to purchase, so grew their list of wants and needs.

Before the 1800s were through, capital had begun to flow across the Atlantic, and America was poised to become, first, the business locus and then the political locus of the world. The 1900s were only half over when Harry Luce dubbed them, quite correctly, "the American century." Soon, though, yet another revolution would take place. Call it the Information Revolution, the High-Tech Revolution, the Internet Revolution—by whatever name, it took business by the neck, shook it, and spread its spirit broadly around the globe.

Today, business drives the world, from all around the world. A global network of corporations, stock markets, banks, and industries churns out more riches than humankind has ever known. Poverty hasn't been defeated. Miseries—from war to disease and famine—spread themselves far too broadly. The environment is threatened, in some cases by the very rapaciousness of the business spirit we are describing. But today, the access to this global wealth and the capacity to participate in the machinery that produces it is available in ways that would have been almost unthinkable even half a century ago.

People have more freedom to be, to do, to go, and to know at the start of the new millennium than they ever have had in the history of time. They have more means and capacity and opportunity to do all those things than the human race has ever known. And in no small measure the credit for that belongs to the business leaders of the previous millennium who have set the table for us all.

How to tell such a tale? In this case, we followed the money to the personalities—both definitive and representative—that have dominated the last thousand years of business, and to some of the most defining and colorful events of the millennium.

Economic power frequently precedes and helps create political power, but business itself is often a trailing indicator of where politics is heading. So it is with business in our own time. The inclusiveness that has come to increasingly characterize Western politics over the last century—of women and of minorities, most notably—has been far slower to invade the ranks of the moguls, the dominating figures of commerce and industry. The history of business exploitation is rich with people from all across the global spectrum, but only recently has the history of business opportunity come to have anything even approaching a rainbow face. Mostly, the story of business is the story of white Western males.

We begin with the story of one such man with whom most readers will be completely unfamiliar: the Englishman Godric, later St. Godric. Why such an obscure figure? Maybe most importantly, because Godric is representative of that relative handful of people who, beginning roughly a thousand years ago, rose up, threw off the circumstances of their birth, and began to freely pursue business opportunity and profit. It would be wrong, perhaps, to claim that such people launched the millennium of business, but it is certainly no exaggeration to write that they served as its early warning system. It was in their persons—their physical beings and in their psyches—that the combination of vectors that would point to economic self-determination were gathering.

Godric gathered his wealth mostly as a seagoing trader across the English Channel and along the newly profitable Baltic and North Atlantic trade routes. Mediterranean traders had it easier in some ways: Markets and ports of call were more established, and the eastern and southern coasts of the great sea of the Middle Earth served as gateways to the exotic goods of Africa and the Islamic world and, beyond that, the empires of the Far East that Marco Polo had brought to the attention of the West.

Even the wealthiest of the merchant traders, though, suffered from the absence of capital markets. Financing a venture, bridging the lengthy interval between the time a ship left port and the time it returned laden with goods—assuming it hadn't broken up in a storm, or been sacked by pirates, or simply run up against one of the myriad forms of bureaucratic disaster that even then plagued merchants—all this required the creation of a modern banking system. And that, as it turned out, took the Italians.

Perhaps it was their own deep involvement in Mediterranean trade that encouraged the breakthrough, or simply native genius. Either way, the Italians seem to have first understood the alchemy of banking. By the mid-fifteenth century, the Italians were bankers to Europe; the city-state of Florence was at the center of the Italian banking industry; and at the center of both—Florence and banking—stood the man who would beget one of the most celebrated family lines in the history of the continent: Cosimo de' Medici.

Born without royal blood, Cosimo would have the power of a prince. As financier to the Vatican, he was also able to strike a bargain reconciling his pursuit of profit with his desire for eternal peace, and the bargain, in turn, would give Florence and the Renaissance some of the most enduring religious art and architecture of the millennium. Money was becoming the great equalizer: Through its exercise on behalf of the public good, even usurers could earn a place in heaven.

Cosimo de' Medici was in his grave less than thirty years when another Italian, Christopher Columbus, set sail for the New World in the service of the Spanish crown—a business venture with an enormous payback. A century and a half later, Spain under Philip II had become the wealthiest monarchy the world had ever known.

Had he been a businessman at heart, one suspects Philip would have known what to do with all the gold and silver that flowed in from his mines in South America. There was infrastructure to be built, both at home and abroad, and markets as well. Spain had virtually no manufacturing capacity: Instead of providing for the needs of its colonies, it had to turn elsewhere in Europe for fulfillment. Spain had to turn elsewhere, too, for the guns and other munitions with which Philip waged a steady succession of increasingly futile wars.

Thus the wealth that came into Spain poured out in a steady stream—under Philip, it never learned to produce wealth on its own—and thus Spain, which had been rich almost beyond belief when Philip ascended to the throne, found itself nearly bankrupt by the time of his death. Not only was money becoming the great leveler; the capacity to handle national wealth was becoming the great discriminator between nations that endured and those that flashed brightly for a moment in time and burned as quickly down to embers.

⤫

No contrast in the dynamics of national wealth could be greater than that between Spain under Philip II and the tiny maritime nation that overthrew Spanish rule just as Philip was dying and quickly established itself as the center of European economic power.

In Spain, economic power had been centralized in the crown. In the Netherlands, money and power were spread broadly across the people. The great Dutch merchant firms— the East and West India trading companies—were funded by public subscription, with the profits flowing back to investors. Just as the Italians had discovered the multiplier effect of banking, so the Dutch discovered the multiplier effect of the stock market. For the first time in European history, national economic decisions were being made by businessmen, not by the crown, a narrow band of rulers, or the Church. The people had available to them, in somewhat primitive form, nearly all the mechanisms we have today for assuming risk in the search for reward, and they were just as free to abuse those mechanisms as modern investors are.

The power of greed to move markets in irrational directions is by now well known, but in the Netherlands in the early 1600s, when the power of greed finally settled on the unlikely commodity of the tulip bulb, the investment bubble that arose was virtually unique. In the opening month of 1637 alone, the price of some of the most prized bulbs shot up nearly 3,000 percent. Then in the first and second weeks of February, the bottom fell out on tulips, and prices plunged even more quickly than they had soared. All across the Netherlands, solid citizens who had gone to bed rich—on paper, at least—woke up staring ruin in the face. Money was not only the great leveler and discriminator; the stock market had also made it the great temptress, a siren that could now infect the dreams of the populace as a whole.

The Dutch empowered the people, and the people learned, ultimately to their great pain, that in a market-driven society, the price of any commodity is whatever investors are willing at any given moment to pay for it. The Industrial Revolution would empower, literally, the world, but for all its consequences, all its resonance through modern history, the Industrial Revolution begins with a simple, almost serendipitous partnership of two deeply different men.

James Watt was, in effect, his own research-and-development team: a brilliant theorizer, an incessant tinkerer, even a superb analyst. Matthew Boulton was very nearly the business ethos incarnate: a born salesman with a keen instinct for numbers who searched restlessly for new markets and new products to turn out at his great Soho Manufactory in Birmingham, England. Apart, unpartnered, neither could have laid claim to enduring fame. Together—with Watt's inventive genius urged on and directed by Boulton's business acumen—they brought about the single most important happening in the world economy.

Steam engines existed before Watt and Boulton, but they were immense contraptions that could move only up and down. Watt figured out how to compact the engine and turn its reciprocal motion into a rotary one, and Boulton knew just how and where to sell a machine that could make things turn. The difference was monumental.

A partnership also empowered the Transcontinental Railroad—this one between government and private interests. The railroad made all the difference, too, and at its core was the rotary power unleashed by James Watt's steam engine, adapted by other hands. The Industrial Revolution had found its wheels.

10

Until the final spike was driven at Promontory Summit, Utah, on May 10, 1869, America—for all its natural wealth of people and resources—was still a nation divided. The Civil War had resolved the political differences that split the nation, or at least had declared a winner, at horrible cost. But it remained for the Transcontinental Railroad to resolve the more epic divisions of time and space.

Getting the rail to Promontory Summit had involved some of the most audacious characters to sidle through American history: men like Thomas "Doc" Durant, Collis Huntington, and Leland Stanford. Congress, which authorized payment for the track laid, had allowed itself to be bribed and otherwise cajoled nearly to a fare-thee-well. But in the end, the railroad got built, new industries and markets sprang up in its wake, and the United States of America was on its way to becoming the strongest economic power on earth. Morality may have been lacking—in Durant's case, it seems never to have been an issue—but as a business proposition, the Transcontinental Railroad made perfect sense.

⤳

Two problems plagued American business development in the wake of the completion of the Transcontinental Railroad. One was a continuing absence of access to the European capital markets: If opportunity sat to the west of the Atlantic, money still resided on its eastern shores. The second problem only compounded the first: The rapid growth of the railroads had let loose an orgy of cutthroat economic competition that further exaggerated capital needs. J. Pierpont Morgan would attempt to solve both.

Working initially with his father, who ran the family bank's London office, Morgan made himself the guarantor of the money that was being sent across the Atlantic. Like Cosimo de'

Medici before him, he knew that everything rested on his word. To assure his word was accurate, Morgan also consolidated— ruthlessly where he considered it necessary—warring industries. For good measure, he also served, in effect, as the central bank of the United States, the lender of last resort in panics and crises. Nine decades after Morgan's death, Federal Reserve Chairman Alan Greenspan grew famous for moving markets with a few cryptic sentences. Famously taciturn, Morgan saved the nation with little more than nods and grunts.

Like other nascent American industries, the oil business was characterized by the fierce competition J.P. Morgan so despised. Unlike other industries, though, oil found its own consolidator already lurking under the tent. The son of a snake-oil salesman, John D. Rockefeller would become the world's richest man and the very epitome of the robber baron—lords of commerce and industry, anointed by their economic power in a time when business called the shots and American government mostly got out of the way. Rockefeller would also give away an absolute fortune during his lifetime and launch one of America's most dynastic, generous, and accomplished families.

Money and power are never simple, but in John D. Rockefeller and the man who would become history's first billionaire, Henry Ford, the two mixed in spectacularly combustible ways. A genius of industrial systems, Ford not only brought the assembly line to automobile manufacturing; he used the assembly line to drive down costs so much that he created a mass market for the cars that rolled off the end. Brilliant. Strangely, though, it appears never to have occurred to him that an auto market of growing sophistication might eventually want more than cheap.

Ford was toasted globally by labor organizations for instituting the $5 work day, which he used to spy on his employees, most notably on any ties they might have to labor organizers. No American industrial mogul has ever come closer to the presidency, especially in the early 1920s when Ford for President clubs were commonplace. He was also highly esteemed by Adolph Hitler for his virulent anti-Semitism, freely expressed in books and the press. Finally, too, for a man who understood the mass market so well, Henry Ford was virtually blind to the power of advertising and image.

Robert Woodruff, by contrast, seems never to have met an advertising medium he didn't like. A college dropout, Woodruff was hired by a syndicate headed by his father to rescue its investment in a nearly 40-year-old Atlanta soft-drink company. In the course of doing so, he oversaw some of the most successful ad campaigns the world has ever known. (Santa Claus's suit is Coca-Cola red for a reason.) Through his advertising, his attention to detail, his messianic zeal, and his product placement— including placement in the hands of American soldiers during World War II—Woodruff also built Coke into the first global brand. Many have attempted to go where Robert Woodruff led them, but Woodruff was there first and, so far, best.

⁓

Like politics, business can make for strange bedfellows. The point is not to fall in love; it's to turn a profit. But even in the pursuit of the bottom line, the merger that brought together an entertainment company founded by a feisty pack of Jewish brothers with a media company launched by the Yale-educated son of Chinese missionaries has to rank among the strangest.

The Warner brothers put sound in film; they invented almost on their own the rip-and-read, gritty movies of the 1930s. In the end, though, they seemed to do more harm to themselves—especially in the warfare between the elder Harry and the brash young Jack—than was visited upon any of their celluloid heroes and villains. Henry Luce, by contrast, would use his stable of middle-brow magazines (*Time, Life, Fortune, Sports Illustrated*—what a genius for titles he had) to both shape

America's image of itself and to tell the nation how to behave, at home and on the world stage.

In the end, after all the principals were dead and gone, their companies would unite to merge content and conduit in what amounted to a royal wedding of the Information Age. How could we not include the Warners and Henry Luce in our story?

And how could any history of money and power across the millennium fail to conclude with Bill Gates? Like Cosimo, he's a king without portfolio. Half Watt and half Boulton, he understood from the beginning both the science and the marketing of software. Like Rockefeller, Ford, and the rogues who built the Transcontinental Railroad, Gates has also never had an aversion to playing tough. And like Woodruff, he knows not just in his bones but deep in his bank account the value of multinational advertising and global branding.

Never before has such wealth resided in one set of hands: $60 billion, $70 billion, $80 billion—every small tick in the share price of Microsoft translates into tens of millions of dollars won and lost. Never before also has such concentrated wealth presaged such a global expansion of opportunity. And there may be the final irony of money and power in this just concluded millennium: that they would concentrate themselves so intensely in the very industry that is extending their grasp to every corner of humanity—even perhaps to some new, yet unknown Godric, waiting for the vectors that will drive the next thousand years of business to point the way.

1

ST. GODRIC
God and Profit

VERYTHING HAS A HISTORY. BEFORE THERE WAS THE Internet, there was the Arpanet. Palm Pilots trace back through laptops and desktops to the 30 ton ENIAC (electronic numerical integrator and computer), which has its roots in the programmable computers invented by the nineteenth-century British mathematician, Charles Babbage. Automobiles were preceded by steampowered tricycles; trains, by wind-propelled land ships. Bankers are the heirs of money changers whose professional ancestors could be found guarding sacred temples used as safe depositories for personal assets.

Great fortunes have histories as well. They are created by visionaries who introduce themselves, their products, and ideas into the proper moment in time, the right crease in history. Henry Luce launched his middle-brow magazine empire just as a huge, and largely homogenous, American middle class was taking shape. Robert Woodruff took advantage of a shrinking globe and a second world war to create the first global brand: Coca-Cola. John D. Rockefeller seized control of the oil refining business just as industry was bursting forth with new energy demands. James Watt and Matthew Boulton launched the rotary steam engine under similar conditions a century earlier.

17

For Spain to grow rich off the mineral wealth of the New World, there had to be slave laborers to dig the gold and silver out of the earth, transportation technology to get the precious metals to the Old World, and a market demand to satisfy. Tulip bulbs could soar to astronomical values in the seventeenth-century Netherlands only because the Dutch had made fortunes in sea trading and had a stock market to condition people to accepting risk for reward.

The transfer of money and power from the cross and crown to the new secular empire of business—the defining change of the last millennium—didn't just happen either. The desire to do business, the impulse to trade for profit, salesmanship born from merchant life—these are instincts nearly as old as the human species. But somewhere around a thousand years ago, a constellation of forces began to pull together in Western Europe.

War, invasion, and conquest, which had ravaged the continent since before the fall of Rome, abated. Until the Hundred Years' War got underway in 1337, Europe was, relatively speaking, at peace. Plague and pestilence subsided, too, and would stay in the background until the Black Death erupted about 1348, eventually killing perhaps one in two people continent-wide. With the coming of political stability, trade began to flourish throughout the Mediterranean and in the north of Europe, around the Rhine River and Baltic Sea. Cities grew and prospered as well, as land-poor lords started to sell off parts of their holdings in the form of town charters. The combination of growing urban populations and growing trade served to concentrate both marketplaces and workforces. Merchant and artisan guilds, which regulated the quality and price of trades, became powerful advocates of self-government.

A hunger for opportunity and personal freedom was awakening at the same time that western Europe began to provide the means for fulfilling individual ambition. The seeds of a business-based economy were being sown. And as that happened a handful of people—pioneers of the rough and tumble economic frontier, bold adventurers in the experiment that would come to be known as democratic capitalism—began to emerge.

⤮

One of first of these capitalist pioneers was the remarkable Godric. Born in the year 1065 near Walpole in Norfolk, in the east of England, he was the oldest of three children of Anglo-Saxon parents. His father, Aedlward, was a freeman who worked a small croft or an enclosed field, on which he most likely grew subsistence quantities of leeks, parsley, shallots, and the like. In return for the holding and the right to work the home farm, Aedlward was expected to render agricultural services to the lord of the manor. He was also dependent upon the lord's stores for food during famine and for protection in time of war—both being ever-present threats.

In the normal course of events, Aedlward's life would have become Godric's, but as a young man Godric aspired to something different, and perhaps even then, to something more. While still a teenager, he left his parents, brother, and sister, and set out to find his fortune. For a time he became a peddler, traveling on foot from market town to market town, selling whatever small wares he could lay his hands on at the annual fairs that were the commercial and social meeting place of the times. Working out of a tent or stall, one merchant might sell hair bought cheap at nunneries for women to add to their thinning locks; others might offer wines or furs. Notaries were available to seal contracts. The rich and poor alike gathered to ogle dancing bears, magicians, and stilt walkers. As they traveled from fair to fair, the peddlers would build a network and, if they had high aspirations, would use their new connections to expand their businesses.

Godric's aspirations soon led him to work as a ship's mate as well as a peddler. Traveling up and down the east coast of the British Isles, he would sell for a profit in the English ports what he had bought cheap from the farmers and craftsmen of Scotland. As his maritime skills expanded, so did his trading network. By age 18, Godric had joined the ranks of the roving merchant-adventurers who led a precarious existence on the margins of the medieval economy, trading freely across the English Channel as they sold ornaments and tapestries to noblemen with a taste for luxury. Instead of answering to the laws and strictures of a lord, as his father had done, Godric was now bound only to the law of profit.

Simultaneously, England itself was emerging as perhaps the wealthiest country in northern Europe. In 1066, the year after Godric's birth, William the Conqueror had defeated the Anglo-Saxon King Harold on the plains of Hastings and thrown the island kingdom into disarray. By 1086, though, William had consolidated his rule so effectively that his agents could undertake a survey of his lands and people that wouldn't be matched for thoroughness for another eight hundred years. The survey results were collected in two volumes that came to be known as the Great and Little Domesday books because the tax judgments rendered from them were as binding on men as God's final judgment on Doomsday.

A national currency system was in effect in England: The monetary term "sterling," used to describe the silver penny introduced by William and his Normans, came into common use just as Godric was leaving home for the first time. Social mobility was possible, too. For a man of Godric's extraordinary, even fierce ambition, there couldn't have been a better time and place, and he was clearly not one to let such an opportunity slip by.

"Thus aspiring ever higher and higher, and yearning upward with his whole heart, at length his great labours and cares bore much fruit of worldly gain," writes his biographer, the monk Reginald of Durham, who got much of the story from Godric himself.

> For he laboured not only as a merchant but also as a shipman... to Denmark and Flanders and Scotland; in all which lands he found certain rare, and therefore more precious, wares, which he carried to other parts where he knew them to be least familiar, and coveted by the inhabitants beyond the price of gold itself; wherefore he exchanged these wares for others coveted by men of other lands; and thus he chaffered most freely and assiduously. Hence he made great profit in all his bargains, and gathered much wealth in the sweat of his brow; for he sold dear in one place the wares he had bought elsewhere at a small price.

As the breadth of Godric's revenue stream grew, so did his net worth, and his potential grew with it. Although born in poverty, he found himself in his early thirties the half owner of a merchant ship and part owner of another. In time, he began sailing south out of England to the ports of northern Spain and then through the Straits of Gibraltar. The novelist Frederick Buechner speculates, in his fact-based but fictional account of Godric's life, that as his budding trading fleet began to reach into the Mediterranean, Godric multiplied his profits from each trip by carrying passengers in the hold—pilgrims bound for the Holy Land or the Vatican in Rome—and by small acts of pirating. Still in his thirties, Godric had become truly rich, a merchant king. For good measure, he even befriended and helped a real king, Baldwin I of Jerusalem, after his defeat in 1102 on the plains of Ramleh. Godric is mentioned specifically in the account of that battle as "Gudericus, pirata de regno Angliae."—Godric, pirate of the English kingdom.

⌐≋⌐

Godric was "vigorous and strenuous in mind, whole of limb and strong in body," Reginald of Durham tells us. He was of middle stature, broad-shouldered and deep-chested, with a long face, grey eyes most clear and piercing, bushy brows, a broad forehead, long and open nostrils, a nose of comely curve, and a pointed chin. His beard was thick, and longer than the ordinary, his mouth well-shaped, with lips of moderate thickness; in youth his hair was black, in age as white as snow; his neck was short and thick, knotted with veins and sinews; his legs were somewhat slender, his instep high, his knees hardened and horny with frequent kneeling; his whole skin rough beyond the ordinary, until all this roughness was softened by old age.

He was also, if Frederick Buechner's *Godric* is to be believed, a brawler and wencher, an especially shrewd trader and, when necessary, a con man and worse. What Godric seems to have been most of all, though, was a man caught in a dilemma. That dilemma—the intersection of values and money, and the search for meaning among conflicting definitions of success— would continue to trouble businesspeople throughout the millennium that Godric saw begin. Cosimo de' Medici bargained with a Pope to resolve it. John D. Rockefeller would bargain with his Maker, while the contemporary global financier John Templeton has spent a fortune encouraging exploration into God's true nature. (Physicist Freeman Dyson, winner of the year 2000 Templeton Prize for Progress in Religion, received a staggering $948,000.) By the millennium's end, a culture obsessed with finding meaning in a world and workplace radically altered by the technological revolution would be rushing to embrace the spirituality of the new age. Godric, though, had no similar range of options. Then as now, a businessman defined his business progress by the profit he made; but then unlike now, the Roman Catholic Church was very clear on which choice Godric had to make. The only true progress was to be found on the road to salvation, and the pursuit of profit inevitably put that progress, and the soul, at risk.

On the North Sea island of Lindisfarne, where St. Cuthbert had once been bishop and where Godric sometimes put in to port during his trading voyages, all the irreconcilable claims on his soul appear finally to have overwhelmed him. The community of monks who lived on Farne invited the wealthy merchant to join them in prayer, and as he did so, Godric was overwhelmed with remorse. *Am I doing the right thing by my fellow man?* he is said to have asked himself, *Am I doing right by my maker? Is this trading deceitful?* Convinced that he was traveling the wrong path, Godric fell to his knees by the windswept shore where the monks lived and vowed to renounce his life as a merchant, a vow he eventually kept with an almost frightening fidelity. Godric's life as a businessman was over.

At age 40, with his sins weighing heavily upon him, Godric left behind his worldly goods and set out to lead the life of a hermit. After walking for many months, he joined a fellow hermit, Elric, at Wulsingham in Durham. After Elric's death in 1108, Godric settled for good at Finchale, on the river Wear near Durham, where he built a small wooden chapel to the Virgin Mary and lived for another 57 years.

At Durham, it is said, Godric mercilessly mortified his flesh in the praise of God. He also developed the gift of prophecy—foretelling, for example, the assassination of Thomas à Becket at his cathedral church in Canterbury in the closing days of 1170—and became a friend of wild animals, many of whom would seek refuge with him when they were being hunted. Even snakes were drawn to him: He kept them as pets, forcing them out of his room only when they distracted him from his prayers. Godric is also credited with being the earliest lyric poet in the English language. One of his works that still survives is a hymn to the Virgin Mary that he set to music. He died shortly before his 105th birthday, on May 21, 1170, and was canonized not long afterward by the Roman Catholic Church.

To the Catholic Church, Godric's transformation is a triumph of spirituality over the misguided values born of a life devoted to commerce. Precious few of us stand so firmly in our principles that we would sell our businesses and give away our riches to save our souls. Nor is it an easy choice to live out the rest of a very long life without earthly comforts, doing penance in solitude. Not only was Godric able to do all these things, but in doing them, he discovered his true gifts: an astounding ability in lyrical poetry and a special communion with animals. By the standards and understandings of the time, the dramatic reversal of Godric's life is proof enough of saintliness.

But Godric's life tells a more complex story than the sainthood he earned. Born at a time when capital accumulation for the peasantry was nearly unthinkable, he was nonetheless a model of modern wealth creation: an up-from-the-bootstraps capitalist who transformed the hand fate had dealt him. In both the major decisions of Godric's life—to pursue wealth and to pursue salvation—he chose to give up the safety and comfort of his known world to pursue at great personal risk goals that might in the end be unattainable. In both circumstances he had to break free of his confines, the perceptions of himself, and the expectations he had been born to. If the second half of his life is a model for the eternal conflict between personal values and the pursuit of prosperity, the first half provides a model as well: of the potential of emerging free-market capitalism to create secular wealth—even for those outside of the upper classes. Business was rising with the new millennium. A new kind of economy was starting to take shape. The pursuit of money and power was just beginning to break free of the politics of the church and the crown, and the Western world would never be the same again.

2

COSIMO *de'* MEDICI
Putting Money to Work

S T. GODRIC MANAGED TO TRAVEL AS FAR AS Jerusalem in pursuit of his business interests, a remarkable journey for someone born a serf in eleventh-century England. Born only 84 years after Godric's death to a noble family with roots in the Dalmatian Mountains, Marco Polo traveled to the edge of the known world, a remarkable journey by any reckoning.

The world was beginning to open up. The eight crusades that were waged between 1095 and 1291 produced only a marginal European presence in the Holy Land. However, even in warfare, they connected the Christian and Muslim worlds, illuminating both. Meanwhile in the Far East, Genghis Khan was creating the largest land empire the world had ever known—larger even than the Roman Empire. In Italy, the establishment of the independent university at Bologna in the late eleventh century was another step down the road blazed by Saint Anselm and ennobled by Thomas Aquinas: Education was beginning to flourish again outside the church. Although no one could have known it, reason had just taken its first tentative steps towards ascendancy.

It was against this backdrop that Marco Polo set out in 1271, in the company of his father and uncle. Just seventeen years old, Marco traveled largely by foot across Turkey and Persia, then along the northern border of Tibet and across the Gobi Desert until, in 1275, the party reached the summer palace of Kublai Khan at Shang-tu (the Xanadu of Coleridge's famous poem). There they would remain for seventeen years, with side trips to Burma, India, and elsewhere, at the bidding of Kublai, the grandson of Genghis Khan and the founder of the Mongol dynasty. In 1292, Marco and company set out for home again, this time by sea around the Malaysian peninsula and up the Indian coast to the Persian Gulf, arriving at Venice three years later in 1295. By then, the ever-observant Marco had amassed one of the most remarkable travelogues of all time, rich with details of his own journey, but rife, too, with a meticulous accounting of the peoples, customs, crops, and other goods, from what was, by far, the most powerful and advanced empire of its day.

Although some of its more flamboyant passages have since been discredited, *The Book of Marco Polo* would help to part the veil that Islam had raised between Europe and the Far East. Before Marco's journey, there had been mostly mystery; with his return and the publication of his observations, there was a fresh understanding of a two-thousand year-old civilization that far outstripped the West in both economic might and scientific innovations. Europeans still moved rocks by hand. Saddles were primitive contraptions. People reckoned direction from the stars and sun. China had wheelbarrows, stirrups for a rider's feet, and compasses to tell commercial travelers and ship captains where they were going, day or night, in sunshine or in rain. Traders working between the Muslim and Byzantine worlds and the West would introduce Europeans to gunpowder, and to far superior technology for making silk, casting iron, printing, and even processing paper.

Innovation and invention have always fueled the ambitions of business people, and Marco Polo's account was no exception. But as the Dark Ages receded, Europe was also beginning to awaken on its own. The urban movement that had begun in Godric's time began to blossom into a multitude of great cities—centers for trade and magnets for commerce generally. As the yoke of servitude was slowly lifted from the peasantry, people who had once spun wool or dyed yarn at home to meet their own needs and those of their immediate neighbors began to gather together to do the same in groups. By centralizing labor, they were able to expand their output; by reducing costs, they could create a profit from their efforts. At the same time, technological innovators were once again learning how to put nature to work.

Little is known of the development of the waterwheel-driven mill in the eight hundred years after the fall of Rome, but by the end of the thirteenth century, the overshot water-wheel had begun to come into wide use. By directing water down a sluice to the top of a geared wheel instead of letting the natural flow of a stream push the wheel from the bottom, mill operators could increase their power, and more power meant more product. A mill powered by an overshot water-wheel near Arles, in France was said to be able to provide enough meal to meet the needs of a population of eighty thousand. Mills driven by horses and cattle were still necessary—water, after all, is subject to drought and freezing—but in ordinary times an overshot waterwheel could do the work of up to five horses, with no diminution of the power source.

Simultaneously, too, another form of multiplying power—the modern banking system—was being born. People learned that if you keep a hundred gold coins locked under your bed, your money is stagnant. Deposit the money with a banker who promises to pay you interest in return, and you have both put your money to work and doubled the amount of money in circulation among your community. Now you have one hundred gold coins and so does the person you've deposited your money with. Let that person lend out the one hundred gold coins to yet another person, in return for an interest payment, and the power of your money has now been tripled, with no diminution of the power source so long as everyone meets the terms of his or her obligations.

Simply put, the more transactions that take place, the richer everyone is, and by the mid-fifteenth century, very nearly the richest person in Europe was the one handling the largest banking transactions of all. Florence by then had become the financial capital of the continent. Its gold florin—so named for the flower (or *florin*) emblematic of the city that was struck on its coins—was the standard of continental currency, the most imitated, and the first, along with the Genoese *genovino*, to be rigidly standardized as to content: Every florin consisted of exactly 3.52 grams of 24-karat gold. The banks of Florence were the standard, too—the places where kings turned to when they needed capital to raise an army, where popes looked to when their revenue streams ran dry, and where even ordinary businessmen with cash to spare could turn a profit by lending their excess out to merchants so they could buy the wares a growing taste for global goods demanded. At the center of the Florentine banking community sat a man who was later to be called *pater patriae*—the father of his country—and whose children and children's children would become the greatest patrons of the arts Europe would ever know: Cosimo de' Medici.

Unable to reconcile profit and his Christian values, St. Godric had abandoned his business pursuits to save his soul. Cosimo would solve the same problem far more simply: by making money and salvation one and the same.

⟫

In the broadest sense, banking is as old as money and the concept of monetary exchange. Because they were held sacred by the people and thus not likely to be robbed, the temples of

Babylon were acting both as safe depositories and as lending institutions as early as 2000 B.C. By the sixth century B.C. the Babylonian Igibi bank was serving as financial broker for companies of traders. Temples again assumed a banking function in ancient Greece, along with private firms that accepted deposits, made loans, and otherwise acted, in a very broad sense, like contemporary neighborhood banks. Beginning in the second century A.D., Roman law provided for notaries to register bank deposits made in payment of debts. Money changing, a critical function among trading caravans and merchant fleets bearing all manner of coin and other specie, dates back many millennia: It was money changers that Christ drove from the temple, in the Biblical account.

Banking died out for much of the Middle Ages because there was so little need of it. Without sufficient business activity, the institution simply withered. The assumption of economic risk, which underlies all banking, depends upon the possibility of economic opportunity. Without one side of the equation, the other can't be completed. With the revival of trade in the late thirteenth and fourteenth centuries, especially trade with the Near and Far East inspired by Marco Polo's travels, banking began to come around as well, most notably on the Italian peninsula.

"Banking belongs to the Italians," John Kenneth Galbraith once noted, and not just the word itself. ("Bank" derives from the *bancos* or benches that Italian bankers sat behind to make their trades.) The city-states of Florence, Siena, Genoa, Milan, and Venice all had substantial interests in vital Mediterranean trade routes that included silk and spice from the Far East and precious metals from mines in Africa, Hungary, and Germany. (In Venice, a combination warehouse-hotel catered almost exclusively to German silver traders.) Where trade flourishes, banking also does, but it wasn't trade alone that swelled the ranks of Italy's banking institutions. The reemergence of pow-

erful kingdoms with economic needs of their own provided a
further spur. By 1330 Italian bankers who had amassed their
assets backing silk traders were helping underwrite royal
finances in France and in England, where Edward III offered
to pay for his loans by licensing the banks to oversee the British
wool trade. When Edward repudiated all his debts in 1339 and
withdrew the license, the effect was devastating for his debt
holders even though most of them lived half a continent away.

A century later, the European banking system was well
established along three distinct branches. The *banchi di pegni*
were essentially pawnbrokers: They made short-term loans to
poorer people in temporary need—the Italian *pegni* is aligned
with 'need.' A petty merchant waiting payment for a shipment
of grain might put up his wife's jewelry as collateral, in return
for enough florins to tide him over until his books were bal-
anced again. Then even more so than now, the interest rates
the pawnbrokers levied were often back-breaking. In fourteenth
and fifteenth century Bruges, in modern Belgium, the *banchi di
pegni* were charging 43.5 percent interest per annum. Elsewhere, the figure is said to have climbed as high as 60 percent.
To combat such rapaciousness, an order of Franciscan monks
in Italy sought and won papal permission in the 1460s to offer
similar loans at only enough interest to cover expenses, through
what were known as *monti di pieta* (pity for the needy).

A step up the pecking order were the *banchi in mercado*, commonly found in the city market area, for which they were
named. In Genoa, such banks operated largely in a loggia in
the Piazza Banchi; in Venice, they had booths along the Rialto.
"The moneychanger-banker or his factor could be found
seated at his table, on top of which he kept a pouch for coins
and an account book for entering deposits and transfers," the
historian Frederic Lane has written. "Pen and ink, an assay
scale for weighing coins and some kind of abacus completed
the necessities of the profession." But if money changing was

a decidedly low-tech affair by today's standards—and if the name itself seems almost invidious in modern times—the money changers were far from trivial cogs in the economy. Like local banks, they accepted deposits, settled business debts, and transferred funds between clients. They also acted as a kind of monetary standardization board, traveling the length and breadth of Europe to assess the true worth of the silver and gold coins minted by a host of city-states, principalities, and lesser and greater kingdoms, all of greater or lesser honesty when it came to accurate representations of the content and purity of their coinage.

At the top of the banking hierarchy were the international banking institutions known as *banchi grossi*, literally 'large banks.' Not for the common trade, the *banchi grossi* moved capital and extended credit across national borders. Through their own widely scattered branches and through correspondent banks, they also facilitated trade both inside and outside borders. Inevitably, the *banchi grossi* dealt almost solely with nobles and with the pope and his envoys, but the exclusivity of the trade didn't radically limit their numbers: By the end of the fifteenth century, thirty-three *banchi grossi* were operating in Florence alone, in part because Florence had spent so much of the first part of the fifteenth century in such need of debt relief.

The great cradle of the Renaissance and the family seat of the Medici—the two are not unrelated—Florence rose to prominence through an almost endless succession of wars throughout much of the first part of the fifteenth century, almost all of them fought by tradition with expensive mercenary troops. War with Milan raged until 1402, at a cost of about 2.5 million florins. (In rough terms, the gold in a florin was calculated to be worth 10 days wages of unskilled labor, 3.5 days work by a skilled artisan, 5 bushels of grain, 4 months rent of a country cottage, or 2 weeks rent of a city home. By such reckoning, the war with Milan ran to about 25 million days of unskilled labor, or roughly

13,700 years of rent on a Florentine townhouse.) The Milanese
strife was replaced by similar strife with Pisa, this time to secure
port access. From 1424 until 1434, Florence was at war with
Lucca. By then, the inflationary pressures generated by rising
wage demands among the mercenaries had driven up costs con-
siderably, to about 3.8 million florins in excess of revenues, or
1.27 million years rent on a country cottage.

To meet its bills, Florence levied a series of almost confis-
catory taxes on its sixty-five thousand or so residents—every
Florentine household was required to file an annual information return listing assets, liabilities, income, family size, and the
like—and on the citizens of the city-states it had conquered
with its for-hire armies. Without an elaborate system of exemptions and deductions, the average Florentine would have been
required to pay taxes that amounted to about 180 percent of
income during the five years beginning in 1428. Even with the
exemptions and deductions, the burden was crushing: Frequent
tax amnesties helped relieve the pain, but the amnesties also
assured that revenues would fall short of needs. As early as
1423, Florence had run up a public debt of about three million florins—six times its tax revenues. (In 1991, near the height
of the U.S. public-debt crisis, the federal debt equaled about
three times federal tax revenues.) To make up the difference,
Florence went to the capital markets, which in the fifteenth century meant going to the *banchi grossi,* and the *banchi grossi* were
only too glad to oblige, at a reasonable return on the funds
advanced. As Edward III and a succession of similarly unreli-
able princes and popes had proved, there was always risk in
dealing with rulers, secular or sacred, and risk demands
reward.

Typically, the *banchi grossi* were structured as partnerships
but run by one dominant family. Today, more than five centuries past their prime, all the banks are gone, and all the family names that once rang with such authority throughout the

Italian peninsula have died out from history except one—the greatest banking dynasty of its time and perhaps the most influential non-royal family in all of European history: the Medici.

⟿

The Medici show up in Florence as early as 1201, when Chiarissimo di Giambono de' Medici was a member of the city's general council, but it wasn't until Giovanni di Bicci, born in 1360 and the richest man in Florence at his death, that the family entered into banking and its fortune became established for good. From there, the name Medici began to spread its way across and through the politics of Italy, the history of the continent, and the culture of the Western world.

Giovanni's grandson, Piero, was a wise and magnanimous ruler of the republic who might have accomplished far more had he not been afflicted with hereditary gout. (He was known as Piero the Gouty, in honor of the family disease.) His son Lorenzo, born in 1449, succeeded Piero and was known to later generations as Lorenzo the Magnificent. A poet and an astute politician, who was to survive both an assassination attempt and excommunication by Pope Sixtus IV, Lorenzo ruled the city during the height of its Renaissance splendor. He counted Botticelli and Verrochio among his friends. When Sixtus IV was succeeded by Innocent VIII, a family friend of the Medici, Lorenzo also arranged to have his son Giovanni created a cardinal at the age of 13. Giovanni, in turn, would go on to become Pope Leo X.

From there, the family tree branches out to include dukes, grand dukes, and cardinals; numerous illegitimate children; an army of political intriguers, some of whom were murdered or exiled for their troubles; and generations of patrons of the arts and learning, including Cosimo II, who would appoint Galileo to the first professorship of philosophy and mathematics at Pisa. There was also a queen in the family: Catherine de'

Medici, who would rule France as the wife of Henry II. Of all the Medici, though, none was greater than—and arguably none the equal of—Giovanni di Bicci's own son, the first Cosimo, later known as Cosimo the Elder.

Born in 1389, Cosimo stayed largely in the background, tending to the bank and other business affairs, until his father's death in 1429. Then he stepped forward with such authority that by 1433 his political rival, Rinaldo degli Albizzi, had him arrested and very nearly sentenced to death. Instead, Cosimo was exiled to Venice for 10 years while Rinaldo set about to try to ruin the Medici *banchi grossi*. After one year of exile, a new government was installed in Florence, and Cosimo was recalled to his home. Rinaldo, who had failed to make a dent in the Medici banking empire, was banished instead, never to return. From then on until his death in 1464, Cosimo's position as Florence's political, social, cultural, and business leader was never seriously questioned.

In recognition of the strong republican leanings of his fellow Florentines, Cosimo never assumed a grand title although he was undoubtedly the Lord of Florence. Politically, he combined the organizational skills of a ward boss with the broad appeal of a populist demagogue. Militarily, he proved himself equally adept at waging war and peace. He prosecuted a successful war against Milan, then turned around and made Milan his ally against Venice and Naples. Finally, in 1454, he negotiated the Peace of Lodi, which put an end to more than half a century of military campaigns and began to free Florence's taxpayers from their burden of debt and Florence itself from the need for the capital markets. In theory, the move should have run counter to Cosimo's own self-interest—his bank had grown fat off Florence—but by mid-century the Medicis had a virtual lock on the papal court as well: One or another of their number had been depositary general of the Apostolic Chamber for more than three decades. Cosimo's close ties to the papacy also gave him great personal influence with leaders of state throughout Catholic Europe, many of whom either had been or would become his clients. Then as now, international banking was just as much about contacts as services.

With his fortune—and it was vast—Cosimo commissioned the sumptuous Palazzo Medici and filled it with works of art specifically created to fit inside: Donatello's great bronze *David*, for example; Fra Filippo Lippi's *Annunciation;* and Uccello's *Battle of San Romano*, three huge panels celebrating Florence's victory over Lucca, which held the place of honor in the palace. Others sculptors, architects, and artists he patronized include della Robia, Brunelleschi, Michelozzi, and Fra Angelico. A bibliophile as well, he assembled a collection of ancient manuscripts and underwrote the construction of the Platonic Academy, dedicated to translating Plato's works and advancing his ideas.

Underlying all of Cosimo's great works, political and diplomatic manipulations, and support of the arts, lay his acumen as a banker. At the peak of the Medici banking empire, Cosimo was overseeing a financial empire that included nine branches, including ones in Geneva and London. In addition to traditional banking activities, the Medicis and their partners were involved in a variety of trade and commercial enterprises, maritime insurance, money speculation, foreign exchange, and what was called tax farming—selling taxation rights owned by a local governing body to a private individual. Without the savvy to maintain control over such a far-flung operation in a time of such plodding communication, Cosimo couldn't have sustained the fortune that supported his largess or his position. As the history of the bank was shortly to prove, it was incapable of running with anything less than the full attention and utter competency of a powerful leader. Only three decades after Cosimo's death, the great Medici bank would falter and disappear altogether, the victim of, among other factors, the lax attention focused on it by Lorenzo the Magnificent.

If the roots of Cosimo's acumen as a banker are complex, at the heart of that success lay a simple proposition: Cosimo de' Medici was trusted. A banker's reputation in fifteenth-century Italy wasn't determined by the financial press or spun by the corporate public-relations staff. It was built on the accumulation of individual acts of fidelity. Sometimes a paper record of a financial obligation would be recorded—the Italians called it a *fede*, or the 'promise.' Far more often, though, financial deals (including complex deals) were sealed with nothing more than a word and a handshake.

For the *banchi grossi* such as Cosimo headed up, the process was always one sided. Their major clients were notorious for inattention to their debts. The banker, though, had no such opportunity: Violate the trust inherent in a transaction—violate the implicit faith—and your reputation would be ruined because more than anything else the whole institution of banking turned upon the simple promise that a banker would do as he said he would do. Skillful in politics and war and admired for his public generosity, Cosimo was most renowned for his honesty and discretion, and both were the basis for everything else.

For Cosimo, there was another part to running a successful bank that was far more troubling. In return for the risk incurred in lending out its own and its depositors' money, banks have to charge some form of interest, be it a specific sum, or percentage of money, or some other calculation of goods or services. Without the interest, there is insufficient reward to stimulate economic activity, and without the activity, the whole pyramid of trade and other commerce that banking supports begins to crumble. However, the Roman Catholic Church was adamant on the subject of interest: To charge anything beyond the principle in the repayment of a loan constituted the mortal sin of usury. Jews were immune from the prohibition—usury was a church crime, not a state one—which in part is why Jews were a well-represented minority among the *banchi di pegni*. For a Catholic, though, to charge interest was to be, by definition, a usurer, and for such a person there was no place to hide, on earth or in eternity.

In some cities, bankers were barred from receiving communion, along with prostitutes. Even where they could take communion, their spirits were often troubled. The records of the early Renaissance are full of thousands of deathbed confessions of interest taking made by bankers and merchants eager to cleanse their souls before Judgment Day. For those who didn't or couldn't cleanse themselves, Dante held out a horrible prospect for their fate. In his *Divine Comedy*, written early in the fourteenth century and perhaps the greatest of all Christian poems, Dante placed usurers in the Seventh Circle of Hell, near the murderers, where they are tortured by a rain of fire.

Like other international bankers, Cosimo and his family sidestepped the canonical law by accepting something other than money in the payment of interest on the loans they made—licenses, goods, services, and other considerations that could be turned into the florins the bank couldn't ask for specifically. When it came to the spirit of the law, though, Cosimo knew he was on shaky ground, and as he grew older, he could feel that shaky ground undermining his prospects of salvation. Finally, overwhelmed with concern about the sin he had accumulated, Cosimo went to Pope Eugene IV and asked him how he could expiate his professional lifetime of wrong deeds. In answer, the Pope and the businessman struck a deal that would have enormous ramifications not just for Cosimo de' Medici and Florence, but for the history of western culture and for the growth of commerce and trade. Cosimo would pay for the reconstruction of the Dominican convent of San Marco, just north of the Medici family houses and one of Florence's most

venerated structures, and the Pope would issue an unprecedented ecclesiastical order: The usurer Cosimo de' Medici was
henceforth formally absolved of all sin. There was, after all, a
middle ground between commerce and canon law.

St. Godric had had no choice in the matter: He had had to
vote for his faith or his business. By the doctrine of charity,
though, Cosimo had been granted safe passage through the
conflict between God and profit, and he was to take full advantage of the opportunity. "Only have patience, Lord, and I will
return it all to you" became one of his favorite and most striking sayings, and return it he did. Over the years that followed,
Cosimo poured hundreds of thousands of florins from his own
private fortune into monasteries, churches, and libraries, and
in doing so, he gave the Renaissance some of its finest work.

For the San Marco convent, Cosimo chose Fra Angelico, a
member of the monastic community there, to paint the frescoes for the ceilings and communal rooms. When that was
done, he had the Medici family parish church of San Lorenzo
rebuilt in the Renaissance style. Soon, he was overseeing the
rebuilding of the convent of the Badia at Fiesole, just outside
Florence; as he had at San Marco, Cosimo had a monk's cell
reserved at the Badia for his own private devotions. The
Palazzo Medici that Cosimo had built beginning in 1445 is said
to have lacked no luxury—"He had neglected nothing which
would add to the comfort of his accommodations," one Florentine architect commented—but its great centerpiece was
the chapel Cosimo had built there, decorated by Benozzo
Gozzoli with frescoes depicting the journey of the Magi. For
his own passage into eternity, Cosimo arranged for burial at
San Lorenzo in a tomb beneath the pavement, immediately in
front of the high altar. For decoration, he commissioned
Donatello to create an adjacent pair of pulpits, one depicting
the Crucifixion and the other the Resurrection. There in
August 1464, he was laid to rest. A year later, the title *pater*

patriae was officially awarded him—the same title that had been accorded to Cosimo's favorite classical writer, Cicero.

Even in death, though, the example Cosimo had provided in life continued to live on. His children and children's children, and his associates and their offspring as well, were to become some of the great patrons of the arts that Europe had ever known, in part for the pleasure of it, and in part because they had learned from their ancestor and friend an important lesson: Capitalism wasn't a one-way street; it was indeed possible to do good while doing well, to both profit and protect your soul. From their patronage and example would evolve the revolution in thought and feeling that today we call the Renaissance. Spurred by the Catholic Church and its canonical insistences, Cosimo helped to create a world that revolved not around God but around a society with man at the center. After five hundred years, power was shifting from the men of the Church to the men of business.

3

PHILIP II
Wealth without Wisdom

UST AS MARCO POLO HAD DONE TWO CENTURIES earlier, Christopher Columbus unleashed the imagination of all Europe when he stumbled upon the tiny Caribbean island of San Salvador on October 12, 1492, and discovered a New World. Here, as F. Scott Fitzgerald wrote of the Dutch sailors who first explored the Hudson, was "something commensurate to [man's] capacity for wonder."

Columbus wasn't the first European to set foot in the Americas. Nor had he specifically intended to get to the raw wonderland where he arrived: He thought he was sailing to the same Cathay that Marco Polo's expedition had traveled to. However, Columbus arrived in the New World at the right moment in history: Behind him stood an Old World ripe with market demand—and equipped with the means of transportation and other technologies to fulfill it. What's more, the New World Columbus had discovered was without any prior claims that would have appeared valid to the average cultured European of the time. Economically, politically, and socially, the New World embodied opportunity: It was a clean slate, waiting to be defined, and it was ripe for the taking.

A European king seeking to claim the wealth of China in 1295 would have had to fight his way through a Mogul empire that stretched from the edge of Europe to the Pacific. One seeking to claim the riches of the Americas had only to defeat indigenous peoples ill-equipped to face down gunpowder and armor. One of history's more profound ironies is that the king who benefited most from the conquest of the New World— Philip II of Spain—was so unprepared to turn his success into a long-term gain.

Columbus's sponsors, King Ferdinand and Queen Isabella of Spain, had their eye on the bottom line from the beginning. They were so convinced that the Great Explorer would find gold that they sent an accountant along with him to begin tallying their wealth. Six decades later, when Philip ascended to the throne, the proof of Ferdinand and Isabella's prescience was everywhere to be seen. Never before had a European nation found itself as rich as Spain under Philip's reign. Thanks to the policy known as the *quinto real*, one fifth of all the silver and gold mined in the brutally won Spanish colonies of Mexico and Peru came directly to the crown, and as the sixteenth century wore on, the supplies of both precious metals seemed inexhaustible. Revenues to the king from the *quinto real* grew five-fold from the late 1520s to the mid-1540s, and seven-fold from then to the early 1590s.

When Philip was crowned king in 1556, he inherited from his father Charles V an empire that included Spain, its New World territories, the Low Countries (later called Belgium and the Netherlands), and half of Italy. Two years before his coronation, he had married Mary I and until her death in 1558 he also served as joint sovereign of England. Philip would add the Philippines (named in his honor) and the throne of Portugal— with colonies that stretched from Africa to India and Indonesia—to his holdings. His would be the largest and richest empire in world history, the first on which the sun truly never set. Yet when he died in 1598, 42 years after ascending to the throne, although Spain's empire was still largely intact its economy was in shambles and its status as a global superpower all but undone. It is clear who was responsible.

A global leader without a global vision, Philip was also a traditionalist fighting the inevitability of change. At the moment in history when there was unparalleled opportunity to build an infrastructure for the future, a time that beckoned great men to dream of the potential of the expanding world— and accept the risks of exploiting that potential—Philip squandered his vast resources trying to preserve the crumbling political order of Spain and Europe's past. Rather than use the vast wealth of the New World to produce wealth on its own, Philip spent Spain's gold and silver so freely on a succession of misguided wars that finally there was nothing left to fall back on. He extracted, rather than built. In the end the gold and silver proved more a curse upon him than a blessing, but if Philip had any particular doubts about the wisdom of his actions, he never showed them.

In fairness, Philip can't be asked to shoulder all the blame. His great-grandfather Ferdinand had created the Casa de Contratacion, or House of Trade, in 1503. By dictate of the throne, all trade with the colonies had to flow through the Casa, which was located in Seville, and had to be handled by Castilians. Naturally, Seville flourished: During the sixteenth century, its population grew fourfold. And like any state-run monopoly, the Casa de Contratacion proved a disaster.

Because the Casa had a monopoly on trade, all requests from the colonies for manufactured goods, for example, had to flow through Seville to Castile. But Castile itself had minimal manufacturing facilities, and almost none of the money that came to the crown was used to bolster capacity. To fulfill demand, the Casa had to import goods from elsewhere in Spain and throughout Europe, at increasingly unfavorable terms. Under pressure from the silver and gold pouring in from the colonies, a general tide of rising prices mushroomed into runaway inflation in Spain in the middle and late sixteenth century. As the colonies grew, demands for manufactured goods soared; to supply them, the Casa had to pay for imports with money rapidly losing its value. Thus, the Spanish crown grew weaker, and the coffers of its enemies grew richer. A state-run Soviet electrical cartel couldn't have been less efficient.

Nor did the penchant of Philip's father, Charles V, for waging war help the Spanish treasury. Philip would inherit his father's obligation to defend Catholicism against heathens and heretics—as a devout Catholic, he probably had little choice. He would inherit, as well, a world in which Muslims and Protestant reformers posed what he saw as a constant threat on his borders. Spurred on by Martin Luther and others, the Reformation was in full swing; the Vatican and Philip meant to stop it. But rich as he was, Philip would also receive from Charles a set of accounting books that would have made a chief financial officer cry out in agony. "Apart from nearly all my revenues being sold or mortgaged, I owe very large sums of money and have need of very much more for the maintenance of my realms," he wrote only shortly after being crowned. "I am greatly distressed to see the state in which things are."

Nor did Philip have anything like absolute monarchal powers with which to remedy the world he found when he assumed the throne. Spain itself wasn't a kingdom in the classical sense, but an association of states, or provinces, that shared a common king but paid allegiance—and tribute—to him to a greater or lesser degree depending on how effectively the king used his royal influence. Control in the more distant reaches of the realm was only as effective as those minions the king sent out to exercise his bidding. Moreover, his power was dependent on his willingness and capacity to exercise force in the support of his rule and policies.

Despite the challenges, Philip still had options: to exercise and enforce power, to win the favor of his constituencies, and to try to control how the new and vast resources were handled. Instead, he made the situation he inherited worse.

Sixteenth century Europe witnessed enormous advances in the arts and science. Copernicus, then Galileo and Kepler, challenged the very structure of the universe. Michelangelo took sculpture to new levels of excellence. In France, Montaigne was inventing the essay form. In England, Shakespeare was born eight years after Philip was crowned and would write nearly half his plays while Philip still ruled. Across the ocean were civilizations no one had dreamed existed 60 years before, forests teeming with game, rivers, it was said, you could cross on the backs of fish.

"I cannot think where this will stop," Teresa of Avila said just about the time Philip was being crowned. "I have seen so many changes in my lifetime that I do not know how to go on. What will it be like for those who are born today and have long lives before them?" Yet at a time when the world was embracing new possibilities, Philip made a fetish of isolating both himself and his country from them. Instead of dealing with the change, both good and bad, that Teresa of Avila fretted over, Philip sought to stop it in its tracks.

History belongs to the winners, and because the Protestants ultimately triumphed in Europe over the Catholic hegemony Philip struggled to preserve, history has long been cruel to him. "Philip was guilty of incest, sodomy, and the murder of his own son Don Carlos," the Dutch revolutionary William of Orange wrote in a memorably scurrilous tract. Others painted him as a warmongerer, a man obsessed with human remains, and a despot only too pleased to burn his subjects at the stake. "If there are vices—as possibly there are—from which he was exempt," the American John Lothrop Motley wrote, "it is because it is not permitted to human nature to attain perfection even in evil." That was written in 1856, 300 years after Philip ascended to the throne, proof that a bad reputation dies hard. Friedrich Schiller would write a play, and Giuseppi Verdi an opera based on Schiller's play, both titled *Don Carlos* and both making dramatic use of the long-standing allegation that Philip had murdered Don Carlos for making love to the Queen, and murdered the Queen as well for good measure.

The truth is more prosaic. The Queen did die, but in childbirth—Philip was to bury all four of his wives and six of his eight children. Don Carlos died as well, under guard and not long before the Queen, but a serious fall in his teen years had left him mentally unstable and subject to suicide attempts. However, the lurid rumors also hint at the isolation Philip lived in and the mystery and secrecy that engendered.

Through his father, Charles, Philip was descended from perhaps the oldest and greatest of all the European royal families—the Hapsburgs. Charles had been a larger than life figure: Holy Roman Emperor (a title that did not pass to his oldest son); a relentless warrior for the church, leading his troops against the infidel Turks and the breakaway German Lutherans. Titian's famous painting shows Charles on a rearing horse, lance in hand and clad in armor. Titian would paint Philip as well—he was a subject of both—but in the equally famous painting of the son, Philip stands indoors with his hand on a table, in what were for him office clothes, with just the hilt of his sword visible, and with a look of arrogance and pride on his scowling face. The difference between the two paintings speaks volumes.

Charles had been multilingual, as befits someone who had so spent much of his life away from Spain with his army. He was, it was said, an approachable man, even a warm one. Castilan Spanish would be the only modern language Philip would master. Apart from a few early forays, he led the troops he relentlessly sent into battle from afar. Philip's biographer Henry Kamen writes that the king "preferred the model of his great-grandfather Ferdinand the Catholic, who commanded armies but did not commit his own person."

As a younger man, Philip had traveled throughout Europe. As king, he ensconced himself in El Escorial, the palace he built early in his reign, high in the mountains outside Madrid. For his pleasure, he filled the Escorial with elegant frescoes and collected books, musical instruments, suits of armor, and religious relics, which included, according to Kamen, "ten whole bodies, 144 heads, 306 arms and legs, thousands of bones from various parts of holy bodies, as well as hairs of Christ and the Virgin, and fragments of the True Cross and the Crown of Thorns."

None of these treasures came without great price, but no one in the world, in theory, had more money with which to indulge himself. Paintings by Bruegel and Bosch (both were also his subjects) hung from the walls. Bosch's grisly surreal scenes were particular favorites. Philip also became El Greco's patron and collected his works as well. Having surrounded himself with so many objects of beauty and contemplation, Philip rarely left the palace and almost never traveled beyond the Iberian Peninsula.

In charge of the most far-flung empire the world had ever known, Philip increasingly ruled it from behind a desk, churning out an endless stream of directives, memoranda, and letters, all in a pinched hand. Except for the most important entreaties, he tried manfully to turn around all the petitions, memoranda, and other documents on the same day he received them. The Spanish empire would become almost as famous for its bureaucratic forms as it was for its conquests. Efficiency seems to have been Philip's modus operandi, as if by cranking the machinery of government he would find some resolution of the larger issues that plagued his reign. Although this attention to paperwork would prove a treasure for later historians, it was a disastrous distraction from true leadership. Like any CEO enisled in his executive suite, Philip grew ever more remote from the real issues that were affecting his empire. As that happened, his youthful reserve and soft-spoken manner grew into something far more fearsome, or, as later historians would write, far closer to depression. Instead of instruction or conversation, visitors had to endure stony silences coupled with a hard gaze and steadily more somber clothing. It was Philip's growing preference for black that gave Europe the "Spanish style."

Such a dark portrayal may overstate the case, or reflect old Protestant prejudices. "Disinclined to speak," Kamen writes in the king's defense, "Philip always felt more at ease expressing himself on paper." But whatever the details, Philip gave Spain a melancholic cast that spread itself broadly over his realm. Instead of reigning over a Spain bright with promise, Philip would become a dark figure in a cautionary tale about how not to lead your people, a study in alienation. In his own family, of course, Philip had much to be melancholic about: the dead wives and children. The Inquisition would give Spaniards much to mourn, too.

~∞~

For eight centuries going back well into the Middle Ages, Spain had been the most religiously mixed of the European kingdoms. Waves of conquest and reconquest between Islamic and Christian forces on the peninsula had turned mosques into cathedrals and cathedrals back into mosques. The long peacetimes that flourished in between had allowed for the creation of a unique culture, with religious balance between worshippers of the Koran and the Bible. Jewish settlements were able to take root and grow strong, too. Obsessed with internal politics, blind to the tremendous economic opportunity laid at their doorstep, and determined to impose religious homogeneity, Philip and his immediate predecessors would change all that, and their tool would be the Inquisition.

As undeniably cruel as the Inquisition was, its horrors can be exaggerated. Few who were brought before the tribunals for falling away from the one true faith were found innocent—about one in five of those prosecuted was absolved—but of those found guilty of heresy, only a relatively low number were burned at the stake. (And, Henry Kamen assures us, Philip never witnessed the burnings.) What's more, in a kingdom that approached a monarchical confederation, the dictates of the Inquisition were not and could not be uniformly applied.

Judged by the terms of what the Hapsburgs had set out to do, the Inquisition could even be declared a success: Jews were expelled or forced into secrecy, and Muslims with them; dissent was silenced. While the guilty were mostly spared execution, they were branded with a stigma that would last for generations, and the Inquisition didn't stop at the tribunal doors. Blood-purity laws reached deeply into the society and ran all the way to the top: Philip was to become deeply interested in the racial origins of his appointees. Study abroad was forbidden in 1558, two years after Philip was crowned. Books were censored as well, and imported books were banned. Finally came word that no book listed in the *Index Librorum Prohibitum* could be printed, distributed, sold, read, or even owned. To escape the restrictions, many educated Spaniards took advantage of lax borders and fled to London and other "open" cities where they could read and write as they wanted. As his father had occasionally done, Philip went after them, authorizing a series of kidnappings meant both to chill the impulse to flee and to return the miscreants to Spain so that they might see the error of their ways. The "reeducation camps" of the Chinese Cultural Revolution come readily to mind.

In neighboring France, Catholics and Huguenots were involved in a bloody rivalry, capped by the infamous St. Bartholomew's Day massacre of Calvinist Huguenots on August 26, 1572. (News of the massacre is said to have made Philip "laugh, with signs of extreme pleasure and satisfaction.") Across the Pyrennes, though, a glum tranquility prevailed, bought at a price that squelched innovation, openness, learning, and industry.

"If these policies were successful from the rulers' viewpoint, in the long run they had quite negative consequences on the development of a public sphere in Spain," writes Victor Perez-Diaz in the June 22, 1998, edition of *Daedalus,* the publication of the American Academy of Arts and Sciences.

> They reduced the plural, diverse nature of society. They encouraged a pattern of dissembling in the sphere of intimate beliefs; strengthened the *takiya*, or habit of dissimulation...and, as indicated in a letter from Luis Vives to Erasmus in 1534, they effectively silenced personal opinion: 'We live in difficult times when we can neither speak out nor remain silent without danger.' Philosophical books and reading came to be associated with dangerous and suspicious objects and activities, thus reducing the frequency, intensity, and freedom of debates in the heart of society on a wide range of matters.

The Casa de Contratacion had given Spain under the Hapsburgs the trading efficiency of a police state; the Inquisition added to that the psychological framework inspired by a Gestapo or a KGB. Nonetheless, Spain remained the richest and most powerful empire in the world, and might have remained so for centuries if Philip hadn't chosen to squander the wealth of the Americas settling religious scores in the Old

World. The imposition of religious homogeneity had sapped Spain from within. Philip II's wars would sap it from without and destroy the economy in the bargain.

Again, there were extenuating circumstances: Every war Philip prosecuted can be justified in terms of the protection of national borders or of his long-standing obligations—of faith and politics—to the Catholic Church in Rome. But kings have choices, and Philip chose to fight and protect the faulty and already dying assumptions of an Old World rather than to build a new, complex, and rich one.

To forestall the Turks, Philip had to defend Italy. If it fell, Rome, seat of the Holy Father, would fall with it, and Spain would have an infidel state practically at its border. Just as bad, the Turks—and the Muslim world generally—were a constant threat along Spain's Mediterranean border. In Muslim Africa too the Turks had a launching ground that history had proved was ignored at Spain's peril. Worse, Turkey wasn't just an abstract threat; in the mid-1500s, Turkey was a superpower with a religious mission of its own.

A massive Turkish assault—three hundred thousand soldiers strong—against the Hapsburg emperor Maximilian's eastern front in Hungary in 1566 died out only because its architect, Suleiman the Magnificent, died in the process. On the sea, a Turkish fleet of some three hundred ships wreaked havoc along the eastern Mediterranean. Philip's cousin, Don Juan of Austria, would eventually deal the Turks a decisive blow at the 1571 sea battle known as Lepanto, a dozen years after the Turks had humiliated a combined Spanish-Italian expedition to seize the Muslim stronghold at Tripoli. For much of Philip's reign, the balance of power was just that: a balance.

Domestically, the Inquisition might have silenced dissent among the Muslims, but driving opposition underground often only sharpens it. During Christmas 1568 a rebellion broke out in Granada, which had been a Muslim kingdom as recently as

1492, the year Columbus sailed for America. Confined at first
to only four thousand *Moriscos*—or Spanish-born Muslims—
the uprising soon spread to nearly thirty thousand troops. By
spring 1569 arms and volunteers were being sent by Muslim
sympathizers in North Africa. Philip's crack troops, meanwhile,
were in Flanders, battling Calvinists in another of the king's
pro-Catholic forays.

In February 1570 the rebel stronghold at Galera fell, all
twenty-five hundred residents were slaughtered, and the town
was destroyed and covered by salt—retribution for Muslim
atrocities that were retributions for Spanish ones. By that summer, the uprising was over, quelled in large part by the mass
import of arms from the factories of Milan. As always, the
arms were paid for with the gold and silver of the New World.
A kingdom constantly at war, Spain never bothered to create
its own arms and munitions industry. The pattern would repeat
itself time and again.

The precious metals of the Americas helped Philip seize
the throne of Portugal when it fell vacant in 1580; otherwise,
there was the threat of a non-Catholic state along the bulk of
his western front. Gold and silver also financed Philip's less
successful incursions into France—a hotbed of heretical
Huguenots. Had he succeeded, Philip hoped to install his
daughter as sovereign. He didn't succeed, though, and more
New World wealth was wasted.

The Low Countries were a particular dilemma for Philip:
a source of great wealth for Spain, yet a hotbed of Protestant rebellion. With the Netherlands, he effectively controlled
the profitable trade routes along the northern tier of Europe;
without the Netherlands, he had only the mineral wealth of
his New World colonies to fall back on. Therefore, he had to
wage war in the Low Countries. If he failed there, he
couldn't wage war elsewhere, and if he couldn't do that, the

Roman Catholic empire and his Catholic kingdom would surely fall.

Obsessed by such domino thinking and entrapped by what military planners call strategic overreach. Philip relied more and more on his gold and silver across the ocean. However, with little reciprocal effort on his part to develop trans-Atlantic trade or to alter punitive tax policies, the New World became a diminishing asset. Even before he had become king, Philip had sided with those who wanted to grant settlers the permanent use of native labor. When that proved insufficient, he approved the seizure of Caribbean Indians as slave labor for the mines, and the import of more African blacks to further augment the slave forces. Still, he spent the gold and silver faster than it could be brought out of the ground. Near-constant war resulted in an imminent threat of bankruptcy. That meant Philip had little time in which to alter his policies toward the New World even if he had had the wisdom to do so. That he had neither a sufficient time frame to act nor the inclination or foresight to do so only added to the discontent of the Spanish settlers in the New World.

"It is commonly said among those who come from Spain, that the officials there are more concerned about ways of squeezing silver from the realm than about how to govern it in the interests of public welfare and peace," Francisco de la Cruz wrote in 1575. A Dominican friar in Peru, de la Cruz went on to fault Philip for "what the king has done with the revenue he has received and receives from Spain and its realms, squandering it and falling into debt." For his troubles, de la Cruz was arrested by the Inquisition, interrogated over three years, and finally burned at the stake, but the larger point the friar sought to make remains unchallenged by history: Granted vast wealth, Philip did everything he could to expend it and almost nothing he could to grow it.

For Philip, a professional career of bad decision making culminated in the worst one of all—the decision to build and equip a vast naval armada for the purpose of invading and conquering England. Once again, too, there was an air of inevitability about the whole affair. Having bought into a failed economic policy in the first place and having dedicated his reign to the restoration of a European order that history was already passing by, Philip seems to have had no choice but to follow both wrong paths to their logical and wrong end.

As the point man of the Counter-Reformation, Philip couldn't sit idly by while Queen Elizabeth reigned in England. Pope Pius V had declared Elizabeth a heretic in 1570, and his successor, Sixtus V, was bound by Pius's papal bull on the subject. So was Philip—the Vatican's champion in the restoration of the true faith. What's more, Elizabeth had been holding the Catholic Mary Stuart a prisoner since the late 1560s. With Mary on the throne in Scotland, there had always been the chance of a natural Catholic succession once Elizabeth died. With Mary in prison for plotting against Elizabeth's life, the chances diminished. With her execution in February 1587, the chances died altogether: Mary's son, James, had taken control of the Scottish throne, but he was Church of Scotland, even more Protestant than Church of England.

Just as important from Philip's point of view, Sixtus had promised him a substantial financial reward once England was invaded, and Spain's treasury was perilously low. Rather than grieve Mary Stuart's death, Philip petitioned the Pope for an advance on his eventual reward.

Early in 1585 word reached Philip that the Englishman Francis Drake, already famous for his pirate attacks on Spanish towns and vessels in the New World, was set to sail for the West Indies with the intent of seizing the silver fleet before it could replenish Philip's coffers. With neither sufficient ships of his own to combat Drake nor the money to buy them, Philip decreed that German, English, and Dutch vessels in Spanish ports be seized and put to the crown's service. When two English corn ships were seized at Vigo, on the north coast of Spain, Elizabeth acted decisively, ordering Drake to bring the ships back and approving his naval campaign across the sea against Spanish holdings there. The two ships had already been released by the time Drake arrived—Philip seems to have realized that he had at least cracked Pandora's box by seizing them—but Drake sailed on to New World at any rate, plundering the Cape Verde islands along the way. Eventually, Drake and his thirty-plus-ship pirate navy would seize and sack Santo Domingo on Hispaniola, the principal Spanish port in the Americas, as well as Cartagena on the South American coast, and Spanish settlements on the coast of Florida.

Financially, Drake's backers took a beating on the expedition. Storms and other delays had thrown off a schedule meant to include sacking and looting in Panama, Honduras, and Havana. Assembled at a cost of sixty thousand pounds, the expedition yielded a return of only about forty-six thousand pounds, once Drake's crew members had been given their share of the booty. In every other way, though, the mission was a success for England and Elizabeth, and a catastrophe for Spain and Philip.

Intimidated by Drake and lacking adequate protection in its home ports—Drake had used captured guns as ballast for the return home—the silver fleet failed to sail for Europe. Almost worse than the loss of money, all of Europe couldn't fail to notice that Drake was already sailing for home by the time Spain assembled a naval expedition to the

New World to chase him. Without precious metals from across the ocean, Philip once again had to seek loans on his own continent, but he and Spain were beginning to look like a bad investment, and the lack of resources was being felt broadly across Spain's overextended empire. In 1585 the Duke of Parma seized Antwerp and seemed on the verge of squelching the Calvinist rebellion in the Low Countries for good. Elizabeth, though, was able to send cash and reinforcements to the rebels; Philip could not do the same to help Parma realize victory. Instead of leading a victorious army, Parma found himself heading up a starving one.

"They are drawing their purse strings very tight and will make no accommodation," he wrote of his efforts to pry money out of Philip. "The most contemplative of them ponder much over this success of Drake."

❧

On May 15, 1586, the following intelligence report reached London from Spain:

> The Bank of Seville is broke:
> > The Bank of Venice also very likely ...
> > General speech that the King of Spain will make a great army for England of 800 sail of ships but as yet is seen but small preparation, and is only a Spanish brag, and very unlikely in many years for him to provide shipping, mariners, and soldiers for such an army unless the French assist him.

The report was accurate in every way but one: Bled dry by his interminable wars, denied access to his cash machine in the Americas, and increasingly seen as a bad credit risk despite holding title to the greatest reserves of gold and silver the world had ever known, Philip had one resource left he could tap: the promised reward from Sixtus V once England was invaded.

Trapped in his own logic, Philip had no choice but to act, and so he did.

Philip received a plan from the Duke of Parma that called for an invasion of England from the Netherlands. Once the Spanish forces landed, they would be assisted by English Catholics. Naturally, Parma would be in charge. From another trusted adviser, the Marques de Santa Cruz, Philip received a second plan. This one called for a huge invasion of England from Spain. Santa Cruz, who would be in charge, put the cost at four million ducats. Even if that figure had been accurate (which it wasn't) it was an impossible sum for Philip to raise. Caught between his two military leaders, Philip devised his own plan, using elements from both the others. The results, of course, are legendary.

Philip's armada of 130 ships left Spain on July 22, 1588, and came within sight of Cornwall at the southwest corner of England on July 29. Nearly two weeks later, a broken armada cleared the English Channel at its eastern end and fled north toward Scotland, the victim of its own inflexible strategy and of a new kind of naval warfare that stressed lighter, more maneuverable vessels. Most of the Spanish ships survived the fighting, but battered by the English pounding and with stores running low, many would not survive the trip home. In all, 51 ships were lost along with thousands of sailors and soldiers: to disease, to exhaustion, and to the rocky western coast of Ireland, where the vessels broke up by the dozens trying to reach fresh water and provisions. England lost no ships and fewer than one hundred men, although as many as three thousand more would die shortly after the battle from a vicious food poisoning.

Philip II would reign for another ten years, dying in his chambers at Escorial on September 13, 1598, at age 71, but Spain would not be the same again after the defeat of its armada. In 1577 Spain's ministers considered but rejected a plan to conquer China—not because it was impractical but because the timing was wrong. Only 21 years later, perhaps not even the dying Philip could entertain such delusions. Gifted with unprecedented mineral wealth, he had set out to reverse the flow of history rather than to look forward and embrace growth, and history has judged him accordingly.

4

TULIPMANIA
Sharing the Greed

PAIN'S CATHOLIC KINGS HAD CREATED THE CASA DE Contratación in Seville and decreed that trade with the Americas be handled only by Castilians in order to ensure that wealth generated from the New World flowed directly to the crown. The result, as we've just seen, was economic inefficiency. By the early seventeenth century, Spain the Invincible had slid into a period of economic disintegration that would persist into the twentieth century.

To bring its far-flung independent traders under a central control and to promote common purpose among them, the independent states of the United Netherlands created the Dutch East India Company in 1602; 19 years later, the Dutch West Indies Company was formed. Instead of vesting all power over the Dutch East India Company in a single authority, a general electorate of 60 members was chosen from among the six local boards that represented all regions of the nation. To spread the risk of sea-going trading voyages that might cover as much as fifteen thousand miles and require half a decade to complete, and to share their rewards, the Dutch East India Company was initially funded by a national subscription that raised 6.5 million florins by selling more than two thousand shares in the company at a cost of about three thousand florins a share.

To maximize the profit potential of each share and of the enterprise as a whole, the company was granted extraordinary powers for a period of 21 years: to coin money, to wage war, to enter into treaties, and to maintain naval and land forces across a vast area that stretched from the Cape of Good Hope to the Strait of Magellan. It was also granted monopoly power over all East Indian trade, as well as freedom from all custom dues on imports. Decentralizing power meant decentralizing authority and decision-making, too. Instead of delays that could become years long as trading ships carried offers and counter-offers back and forth between sultans and authorities in the Hague or Amsterdam, the Dutch East India Company's governors in the field were empowered to take action when and where needed.

The result: Wealth was shared, and trade boomed from Capetown to Sumatra. Instead of crusading for God as Philip II had done, the Dutch traders crusaded for what has mattered to traders throughout time: profits. In the lucrative East Indian spice trade, they found a perfect medium for their aspirations: Nutmeg, cinnamon, cloves, and other spices bought cheap in the trading ports of the Indian Ocean and South China Sea brought ten times their purchase price in the marketplaces of Europe. Less than a half century after wresting its independence from Spain and Philip II, the Netherlands, still a tiny maritime nation of just two million people, had become the richest country on earth.

Just as economic policy in England was increasingly being set by a majority of merchants in Parliament, so economic policy and practice in the Netherlands fell not to potentates but to businessmen. And where business reigns, business is often good. The seventh voyage of the British East India Company (which had been established two years before its Dutch counterpart) yielded what even today is an enormous return on investment for shareholders: 214 percent on an original outlay of a little more than fifteen hundred pounds sterling to support the 1611 to 1615 voyage. At the height of the Dutch East India Company's power in the late 1660s—when it had 150 trading ships at sea, 40 war ships to protect them, and some ten thousand soldiers—investors were earning annual dividends of 40 percent, and sometimes in excess of 60 percent. For the first 94 years of its existence, until 1696, the company's annual dividend never fell below 12 percent.

It wasn't just in distant maritime trading, though, that the Dutch adopted a model strikingly similar to today's equity markets. Shares in what were known as joint-stock companies, the forerunners of today's publicly traded corporations, were bought and sold at the Bourse, named for the courtyard of the Amsterdam *Beurs*, one of the first stock exchanges in history. The Bourse opened promptly at noon and closed promptly at two on trading days. If the market lacked modern electronics and ticker tapes, its rituals would still feel comfortable to any trader who has ever spent time on the floor of the Chicago Mercantile Exchange. Offers were made by manual amplification—that is, shouting—and buy and sell bids were sealed with a slap of the hand. Instead of being shut out of the nation's economic life, as Philip had shut out nearly all his subjects in Spain, Dutch burghers were invited in, and they became acclaimed for their skill and prudence as investors.

Banking had multiplied the amount of money in circulation by putting the same funds to work at multiple points. The invention of these protocorporations did the same thing with risk and opportunity. Large enterprises grew from the aggregation of many small risks; large rewards, if and when they happened, were aggregated broadly across the burgher class. In theory, it should have been the economic equivalent of a perpetual motion machine. In practice, every new wrinkle in the economy breeds its own excess, and the Netherlands would prove no exception. The downfall in this case can be laid squarely at the feet of one of nature's beautiful creations and one of mankind's most enduring emotions: tulips, and greed.

In Dutch, it became known as *Tulpenwoede*—Tulipmania— and to the extent that anything so complicated can have a single beginning, this one began in 1551 when the Viennese ambassador to Turkey, Ogier de Besbeque, paid a visit to the Turkish trading center at Adrianople (now Edirne), almost due west of Constantinople along the border with Greece. Before the year was out de Besbeque would write to Vienna of the unusual flower he had seen there, notable for its long stem, cup-shaped blossom, and silken petals. Soon, he would follow his letter with seeds, and a new horticultural industry would begin to be sown across Europe. The first printed description of the tulip, including illustrations, is credited to the great Swiss naturalist Conrad Gesner, in his *De Hortis Germaniae*, published in 1561. The following year, a shipload of tulip bulbs arrived in Antwerp (then a part of the Netherlands) from Constantinople, to considerable excitement.

The uniqueness of the tulip alone would have been enough to generate interest: Inspired by Marco Polo and others, Europeans had been intrigued by exotic imports from the Near East and Asia for more than two centuries. But tulips have one more botanical property that helped put the craze over the top. In their natural state, unaffected by disease, tulips occur in solid colors, indeed in every solid color except true blue, from pure white to an almost-black deep purple. Attacked by a mosaic virus, though, tulips do what is known as breaking: The natural color becomes broken by irregular streaks, and the bulb, once infected, will continue to produce flowers of the same pattern year after year. Find a broken pattern that you especially like, and you can plant bulbs that would otherwise produce solid-colored flowers in the same soil and have them repeat the now-regular irregular pattern within a few years. Or you can propagate the broken pattern by breaking bulbets off the main bulb and planting those—the virus itself does no harm to the bulb or its longevity, only to the regularity of the flower's coloring. Thus, tulips were not only unique in their own right; they constantly and naturally spun off fresh uniqueness, and the most successful new strains could be preserved and multiplied.

Originally a fad, tulips were soon the subject of a growing demand; and with a supply chain as long as that of tulips in the mid- to late sixteenth century, demand quickly created scarcity. It wasn't long after the first shipment of bulbs arrived in Antwerp that demand for tulips began to outstrip supplies. As that happened, prices rose, and as prices rose, tulips began to assume an economic value out of proportion to their intrinsic worth. Inevitably, domestic cultivation of tulips flourished, and the price of the most common solid-colored varieties fell. But domestic cultivation also produced more and greater "broken" varieties, ironically driving up the value of uniqueness.

By the start of the seventeenth century things had gotten so out of control that single bulbs of new tulip varieties were considered acceptable dowry payments for brides in many parts of western Europe. One story tells of a French businessman who exchanged his flourishing brewery for a bulb of the variety Tulipe Brasserie. But what was true generally of Europe struck with special force in the Netherlands. Part of the reason was simply the onset of mass hysteria: In a small, relatively closed, and homogeneous society word travels fast, and greedy impulse always feeds the fear of being left behind. The panic— the mania—that was to take such root in Holland, though, had deep and varied roots of its own.

Geology, for one thing, favored the Dutch. Tulips flourish best in sandy, well-drained soil, and for eons, the old mountains of Europe had been eroding into sand and flowing with the waterways of the Rhine out to the Low Countries. Large tracts of the Netherlands were a tulip field waiting to happen when tulips finally arrived in western Europe.

For the Netherlands, political and social history, and the madness for tulips, met at the right moment, too. Dutch maritime traders were already raising the general level of prosperity of the country and the people by the time the Netherlands won its independence from Spain in the late 1500s. Bitter religious wars would punctuate the decades ahead, including a brief reascendance by Spain, but by the start of the 1600s, Amsterdam—long one of the principal trading centers of northern Europe and happily free of much of the sectarian strife—would be ready to lead the Netherlands to continental ascendance.

Across the Channel, the Golden Age of Elizabethan England had been marked by great writers, Shakespeare foremost among them. In the Low Countries, the Golden Age was marked by great painters, and great painters in profusion always suggest great wealth and patronage to support them. Among Dutch painters, Frans Hals, dean of what became known as the Haarlem School of painting, was born in 1580; the great Rembrandt, in 1606; Pieter de Hooch, in 1629; and perhaps the most technically accomplished of them all, Jan Vermeer, in 1632. Next door were the Flemish giants: Peter Paul Rubens, born in 1577, and Anthony van Dyck (1599).

Amsterdam itself became the outward and visible manifestation of the nation's mounting riches: Beginning in 1612, the town was ringed by the Buitensingel, a moat with 26 bastions. Within, a secession of memorable buildings were soon being raised: the Mint Tower, built into an old medieval gate; the Westerkerk, or West Church, with its 282-foot tower, where Rembrandt is buried; and the town hall, now the royal palace.

In a lesser but far more pervasive way, tulips also became an outward and visible sign of mounting riches. Had they been merely pretty, tulips might well have graced many Dutch gardens. But their beauty came at an increasingly steep cost, and thus tulips not only pleased the eye but became tokens of prosperity and measures of prestige—both nationally and individually. A country that could afford to so indulge itself was indeed wealthy and so too was any citizen who could so bedeck his own property. An expansive tulip patch, a party in a conservatory decked out with tulips, even window boxes lavishly decorated with tulips, became a way of announcing social standing, like country club memberships and the number of Mercedes in the driveway.

⚜

Nations, of course, survive fads all the time. The Netherlands, though, had in abundance a third and vital component for feeding the coming mania: a propensity to trade in the pursuit of profit and a tolerance for risk.

At the low end of the risk spectrum, Dutch investors of the early 1600s could put their money into publicly regulated banks or insurance companies, or they could invest it in the trade through the Baltic Sea, effectively a Dutch monopoly. Such investment routes and instruments were the Treasury notes and corporate bonds of the day. The two "Indias"—the Dutch East and Dutch West trading companies—offered the promise of much higher return, especially the Dutch East; but that had to be set against the higher risk inherent in distant and perilous travel and the great time lag between investment and payout. "Daytrading" in voyages that could take years to complete was neither prudent nor possible.

If the Dutch East and West trading companies were the IBMs and General Electrics of their day, the Bourse was much closer to a combination of the young NASDAQ and the Chicago commodities market. In addition to all the risks of moving rapidly in and out of investment positions, the Bourse offered what were, in effect, stock options and futures trades. Inevitably, too, it attracted short-sellers and manipulators who attempted to drive down prices through the spread of negative news and rumors. As early as 1610, edicts had been issued proscribing a whole variety of shady activities on the Bourse, most notably the practice of *windhandel*—that is, "trading in the wind," or dealing shares not in the possession of the seller. If the Dutch had come a long way from the days when the accumulation of any excessive profit was considered godless, they seem to have drawn the moral line at profiting without anything in hand. Tellingly, though, there was no prescribed penalty for such futures trading: Contracts were simply deemed to be legally unenforceable. Private enforcement mechanisms allowed for unlimited futures trading for those who were willing to work without the net of official sanction.

It was this tension between safe and speculative investment that both sustained and nurtured the Dutch economy. Safe investments in banks and the Baltic trade created value; speculative investments on the Bourse spawned growth. In between the two extremes, the trading companies acted as an even keel keeping the ship on course. And it was this tension that tulips were to so upset.

The more people became interested in attaining wealth and growing it rapidly, the more they turned to the high-risk model of the Bourse, both in Amsterdam and at its regional locations throughout the country. And the more tulips came to be treated not as flowers but as assets—that is, the more their extrinsic value became divorced from their intrinsic use and worth—the more happy and anxious people were to trade in them. By the 1620s the best banks in Amsterdam were boasting tulip vaults. As befits any good and valuable asset, bulbs could be used to secure loans, and the rarer the bulb, the greater the surety offered. There were even rumblings of going off the gold standard and on to a tulip one.

Increasingly, as the 1620s drew to a close, the tulip sector
dominated the entire Dutch economy. Among a people already
conditioned to assume risk in the pursuit of reward, there were
fewer and fewer places left to turn. As the frenzy mounted,
there was also no other place that offered the promise of such
returns, and thanks to the endless inventiveness of capital markets, there were also constantly expanding opportunities to pursue return. Tulips offered one further advantage: Unlike gold
or diamonds, they didn't have to be dug out of the ground in
distant climes, and unlike stocks in joint-share corporations like
the Dutch East India Company, they weren't out of the range
of the average working man. Common bulbs, those that produced flowers of solid and common color, were relatively inexpensive, and while they had little worth in the state they sold
in, there was always the hope that a mosaic virus would break
the color in a unique, and uniquely valuable, way. The Bourse
traders had conditioned the populace to the equations of trading and to the psychology of the trader, and the populace had
learned its lesson well. Common bulbs weren't quite the penny
stocks of the Tulipmania—they cost more than that—but they
provided a point of entry for would-be traders and speculators
who had previously been shut out of the action. For building
a bubble economy, there couldn't be a much better plan.

A possible fourth contributing factor to *Tulpenwoede* needs
mentioning as well. In a paper delivered to a Salomon Brothers conference on market crashes and panics, University of
Providence economist Peter Garber writes: "External to the
bulb market, one important event in the period 1634–37 may
have driven the speculation. From 1635 to 1637, the bubonic
plague ravaged the Netherlands." More than seventeen thousand died of the plague in Amsterdam in 1636 alone, Garber
notes, a seventh of the population of the city. In Leiden, it was
even worse: One in three people died in 1635, more than fourteen thousand five hundred in all. In Haarlem, then (as now)

a center of the tulip trade, and perhaps the epicenter of *Tulpen-woede*, one in seven people died in four horrible months alone, despite drastic health measures.

"These and other precautions could not prevent the progress of the outbreak that caused 5723 to die during August, September, October, and November 1636, so many that the number of graveyards was too small," one Haarlem historian cited in Garber's paper writes. "So great was the misery and sorrow of citizens and inhabitants that the best description would only be a weak image of the great misery of those unhappy days. . . . In the midst of all this misery that made our city suffer, people were caught by a special fever, by a particular anxiety to get rich in a very short period of time. The means to this were thought to be found in the tulip trade."

Whatever the causes of the mania—and even allowing for some exaggeration in the historical accounts that came down to us—the simple fact is that beginning in the mid-1630s, the people of the Netherlands pretty much took leave of their senses where flowers were concerned. As tulips came to dominate public consciousness, more and more of the agricultural life of the country was taken up with planting and cultivating them, more and more of the social life of the country was taken up with the status power of tulips, and more and more of the economic life of the country was taken up with buying and trading them. As the latter happened, the markets expanded in sophistication to satisfy demand.

Tulip analysts and consultants made a nice business in parsing stem quality and pigmentation. Tulip "riggers"—what British writer Rhymer Rigby calls "the Ivan Boeskys of their era"—meanwhile tried to drive the market by manipulating demand. "A typical tactic was to invest heavily in bulbs from an area, then have cattle stampede those fields to create a shortage," Rigby writes in the June 1997 issue of *Management Today*. "One peasant, having grown a rare black tulip, sold it for 1,500 guilders to a trader who promptly crushed it underfoot. Such measures, explained the trader, were necessary: He, too, had a black tulip and would cheerfully have paid up to 10,000 guilders to protect its singularity and price." Ten thousand guilders, it should be noted, was a near fortune. Rigby goes on to tell the story of a farmer, bankrupted when a cow ate its way through his tulip patch, who tried to recoup his fortune by creating a market in "tulip-milk" futures.

At the height of the frenzy in 1636 and early 1637, one man was said to have traded several acres of prime farmland for a handful of rare bulbs; another man, his house for the same. A wealthy merchant apparently paid 2,500 guilders for a single Viceroy tulip bulb—equivalent to the annual output of a good-sized farm. A single Semper Augustus bulb went for more than twice that.

Professional tulip traders continued to deal with one another, and to reap the benefits of the boom, but beginning in about 1634, amateurs flooded into tulip trading. Foreign capital followed in 1635 and 1636, and the combination of the two—new money and a vast pool of new players—seemed to bring the tulip market to critical mass. Throughout the Netherlands in every strata of society, people began liquidating their assets in order to be able to participate in the boom. By then, Garber writes, the trade in tulips had separated into "piece" and "pound" goods.

Piece goods—rare and highly prized flowers—sold by the bulb weight, with contracts specifying both the particular bulb and the site of its planting. For the most part they were the blue chips of the tulip bubble market, bought and sold by moneyed interests. Pound goods—the cheaper, common bulbs—sold by the lot and could come from any stock and any location, and as the market swelled and the second-tier players came tumbling in, it was the pound goods that most benefited. The price of piece goods had risen steadily—tripling over the course of several years. By November 1636, the action had moved to pound goods, and as it did, they raced to catch up with their exquisite cousins. In the first month of 1637, the price of pound goods multiplied as much as twenty-five times. By then, there was no need for an actual tulip on either side of the trading equation.

By their very nature, tulips had a truncated trading season: They bloomed in the spring, and the flowers would bespeak the quality of the bulbs and their offshoot bulbets, which would then be harvested by late summer and sold off soon thereafter. But that was only if you dealt with what actually existed—with actual bulbs and actual guilders. If you extended the trading season to trade what you didn't currently possess and in fact never intended to possess, you could trade year round. This happened to the tulip trade. A futures market in bulbs began to develop in the Netherlands early in 1636. By summer, the trading in futures became so intense and extensive that groups of traders began meeting regularly in taverns, in what became known as colleges.

Tulip futures contracts commonly involved neither cash on the barrel head nor tulips in hand; nor was there any expectation of delivering an actual bulb on any actual date. (Nor, for that matter, was there any notarization of the terms—deals were commonly sealed by the payment to the seller of a fractional sum of the arrangement known as wine money.) Just as futures contracts in our own time are buyer bets on the eventual fetching price of pork bellies and petroleum, not offers to purchase a train-car load of pig parts or crude oil at some specific date, so the futures contracts on tulips were buyer bets on the eventual fetching price of the bulbs. Like all futures markets, the one in tulips was also—at least on the surface—a way to offset the existing risks of the business for the seller: If the price rises beyond what you agree to provide the commodity for, you lose; if it falls, you win; but either way, you know what to expect.

Futures trading assumes a rational market, but by the summer and fall of 1636, any last vestige of rationality had long fled from the Dutch tulip market. Instead of betting on the eventual price of tulips, investors were betting on the Greater Fool Theory—that is, that there would always be someone further down the road willing to pay even more than you had paid for a product the price of which had become completely disconnected from any intrinsic worth. Somewhere between February 5 and February 6, 1637, four years after the Tulip Mania began in earnest, the Greatest Fool was finally found.

Typically, bubble economies collapse in a heap—that's where their name comes from—especially in the absence of a strong central authority to cushion the fall. Manias create their own logic, but at the very moment the last fool gets into a mania market, everyone else seems to suddenly realize that the potential for risk so greatly outweighs the possibility of reward that it's time to cut and run. In the Netherlands, in February 1637, the tulip traders cut and ran in droves.

Peter Garber estimates that the price of a White Croonen tulip bulb had risen 2,600 percent during January 1637. By the end of the first week of February, it had lost 95 percent of its peak value. Switsers, another common bulb, appear to have lost two-thirds of their value in only four days, between February 4 and February 9. Nor would history offer much redemption for those who had overpaid. Records show that an Admiral Liefkens bulb had sold for 2,968 guilders on February 5, 1637; 85 years later, in 1722, Admiral Liefkens were commanding .2 guilders on the open market.

For the Netherlands, the collapse was devastating: A people who had risen to the crest of prosperity by sharing the opportunity to amass wealth and by aggregating and spreading risk had lost their bearings in the face of a simple flower. No risk, they had learned, equals no reward. What they seem to have forgotten was that all risk equals no reward, too, once the Greatest Fool is found.

Moneyed burghers who had purchased rare piece-good bulbs as prices soared in the final weeks of the bubble found themselves in possession of utterly wasted assets. It was as if they had bought a 24-carat gold hula hoop on the last day of that fad, but at least a gold hula hoop would have had melt-down value. All you could do with a radically devalued bulb was plant it and enjoy the brief annual flower. The poorer Dutch who had been trading in futures contracts on common pound-goods bulbs fared no better without a further and greater fool down the purchase chain to relieve them of their obligations.

Nor were local governments much inclined to offer relief. Having taken their stand with Bourse officials that futures trading was, if not evil, then at least morally lax, officials generally let the pain fall where it would. Haarlem did pass a regulation that said buyers could settle their contracts on payment of 3.5 percent of its price, but the contracts themselves were so legally suspect that many buyers just walked away from them. Sellers who had assumed great debt in expectation of grossly inflated future returns still had their debt, but they had little recourse to climb out from under it. Ordinary men and women who had gone to bed on the night of February 5 thinking they were rich woke up penniless, forced into workhouses to pay off their debts, and those ordinary people collectively formed a substantial part of the adult population.

⁓

For the market moralists, *Tulpenwoede* would prove a field day. In the years directly after the panic subsided, the Netherlands was flooded by pamphlets cautioning against such high-risk economic behavior and urging the Dutch instead to put their money into lower-risk, lower-return instruments. (The pamphlets seem to have been backed, at least in part, by the directors and beneficiaries of those lower-risk, lower-return instruments.) In the centuries to come, *Tulpenwoede* would frequently be invoked whenever it seemed that mass hysteria had driven prices out of whack. Even in the twentieth century, Bernard Baruch had lobbied hard for the re-issue of a nineteenth-century history of the Tulip Panic as a way of teaching the investing public about the role of crowd psychology.

Humans, though, are a hard-headed lot. Less than a century after the Dutch bubble burst, the British saw their own version—the South Sea Bubble—explode. In the summer of 1720, stock in the South Sea Company, which held a largely useless monopoly on British trade with South America and the Pacific, climbed to £1,000 a share. By December, the price had fallen to £124. Not to be outdone, the French earlier that year had run up the price of land in the Mississippi River Valley to insane, and completely unsustainable, levels. Two centuries later, land bubbles were still building, and bursting. Crowd mania has even made its way into fiction. George Webber, the protagonist of Thomas Wolfe's famous novel *You Can't Go Home Again,* falls into the middle of real-estate mania on the eve of the Great Depression when he tries going back to a thinly veiled version of Wolfe's own hometown, Asheville, North Carolina. And in the present, the new millennium began with shares in high-flying high-tech businesses like priceline.com losing more than 95 percent of their value in months, not years.

In a market-oriented society, people can drive up the price of any commodity—from tulips to impressionist paintings to IPOs—to levels that cannot be rationally justified. Value, after all, is defined finally by time and place, by what someone is willing to pay, not by what something is inherently worth. For a relatively few short years in the time of the seventeenth century, in the place known as the Netherlands, the people who make up the market decided that tulips were akin in value to the purest gold.

5

JAMES WATT *and* MATTHEW BOULTON

Turning Evolution into Revolution

Y THE CLOSING DECADES OF THE EIGHTEENTH century all the elements were in place for an industrial revolution, save for one. Improvements in agricultural production and in the storage and transportation of food meant that for the first time in human history, average people could live at a significant distance from basic food sources. In Western Europe, urban populations had begun to explode. London was nearing a million residents. Paris had started the century with a population in excess of six hundred thousand. More people living more closely together also meant a concentrated work force and, just as important, a concentrated marketplace.

As we've already seen, banking and finance generally were passing beyond adolescence into a maturity at least beginning to resemble the sophisticated capital mechanisms of today. A stock market had been in existence in Amsterdam for nearly two centuries. Capital wasn't the problem, or capital structures. Nor was there any absence of facilities for manufacturing. The use of the word "factory" to indicate a building for the production of goods dates back to 1618. "Industry," in the sense of systematic work or labor, had entered the English language seven years earlier. People in short, had already begun to acclimate themselves to the habits of time management and repetitive work that the coming century would so magnify and ingrain.

Of all the nations of western Europe, none was more primed for change than England. France had the greater capital—despite losing much of its empire, it was still the richest nation in Europe—but Great Britain had the better monetary system and lower interest rates, and it was governed by a Parliament that, because it was controlled in large part by commercial magnates, favored legislation that promoted the growth of business.

England also had in abundance what other European countries had only sporadically: an industry ripe for revolution and one predisposed to technological innovation. It was geography that gave textile manufacturers their leg up in England: The moist air served to make the thread more supple and less likely to break than in drier climes. But it was native inventiveness that had caused the textile industry to grow so rapidly during the middle half of the eighteenth century. John Kay's flying shuttle dramatically increased the speed with which weaving could be done. James Hargreaves's spinning jenny, introduced three decades later in 1769, meant spinners could finally keep up with weavers.

What was missing from this picture—what was needed to jump start this evolution into a revolution—was a cheap and reliable source of power, a way to turn the machines more quickly so that more goods could be produced in a briefer time frame and thus market demand could be both increased and served, and economies of scale could be achieved. For that to be found required an almost serendipitous meeting of two radically different men and the wisdom in both to see that the other offered the fulfillment of a dream.

James Watt is known to us as the father of the Industrial Revolution, and indeed the steam engine he brought to such perfection is *the* defining invention of the movement. Yet without Matthew Boulton, it seems likely that Watt would have wandered through the wilderness of history as a kind of real-life Gyro Gearloose, a brilliant mind without the necessary practicality to turn his brilliance to utility. He needed to partner in order to transform his genius into a product and to bring the product to a market where fortunes were waiting to be made.

Matthew Boulton almost disappears from history, and indeed, without James Watt he would have been just another very rich and admired man of his time, hardly worthy of note by future generations. But it was Boulton who took Watt and his steam contraption in hand, Boulton who knew almost intuitively the potentials in Watt's work, and Boulton who unlocked the utility in Watt's genius so both men could profit from it.

Had Matthew Boulton and James Watt never met, the Industrial Revolution certainly would have come about—too many forces were pointing in the same direction to have missed it—but who knows how long the revolution would have been delayed. But Watt and Boulton did meet, the steam engine was launched, and with it began something remarkable: the single most important happening in the history of the world economy.

⟜

On July 4, 1776, the first Continental Congress, meeting in Philadelphia, approved a Declaration of Independence from England and began to rewrite the history of global wealth and power. Four months earlier, on March 8, 1776, a crowd gathered in Birmingham, a little more than a hundred miles northwest of London, saw the first public demonstration of a machine that would prove, once it had been refined, to be a declaration of independence from running water. No longer would factories be held ransom to the vagaries of drought or freeze. No longer, for that matter, would industries have to locate themselves on the banks of rivers or streams. Power would come to them, in the form of steam, instead of their having to go to the power source. And what muscle this new power had: Even the relatively primitive steam pump being put through its paces that day could do the work of a hundred men. No one who witnessed the moment could have possibly known it—such moments always get designated in retrospect—but the right man and the right idea had just intersected with exactly the right moment in history, in just the right place, to give birth to the Industrial Revolution.

The machine that James Watt demonstrated March 8, 1776, was far from the first steam-powered engine. A hundred years before Watt began his tinkering, Edward Somerset had produced an "atmospheric engine" that helped establish many of the broad principles of steam power. In 1698, Thomas Savery had obtained a patent for what's generally considered the first practical steam engine, one capable of raising water, and for several decades afterwards, Savery's engine was put to wide use—to pump water out of mines, for example, where it pooled from underground streams, or to supply towns with water, or drive waterwheels for factories. Savery's engine would be supplanted by Thomas Newcomen's, the first steam engine to use a piston and cylinder, and Newcomen's, in turn, would become the standard in England for the bulk of the eighteenth century. Savery and Newcomen's engines, though, suffered two defects: Both were huge, as large as four-story houses, and thus imminently unportable, and because they used heat so inefficiently, both were enormously wasteful. Even the mining companies that dug coal had trouble affording the coal the engines needed to burn to keep the mines dry.

James Watt would solve both problems, increasing not just the power of the steam engine but multiplying its utility, too, and in doing so, he would change manufacturing forever. But for all that to happen required a convergence of circumstance.

Born in Greenock, Scotland, on January 19, 1736, Watt seems to have been both high-strung—he was subject to migraines his whole life—and fragile by nature. His paternal grandfather, Thomas, had been a teacher of surveying and navigation; his father, James, was a shipwright and both a maker and supplier of nautical instruments. Scientifically inclined himself and a perfectionist in his work, Watt learned craftsmanship in his father's shop before going off to London, at age 19, to apprentice himself to a maker of scientific instruments. A year later he was back in Scotland, worn out by his apprenticeship and by the mean living conditions it subjected him to. In Glasgow, now all of 20 years old, he tried again to set himself up as an instrument maker, but the local guilds would hear nothing of it since Watt had failed to complete his apprenticeship tour in London.

The first big break of James Watt's life came a year after his rejection by the guilds when Glasgow University—more interested in the young man's talents than his credentials—appointed him "mathematical instrument maker" to the University. Watt soon became close friends with a chemistry lecturer at the university named Joseph Black, who later discovered latent heat, and also with an undergraduate named John Robison, who went on to a distinguished professorship in natural philosophy at the University of Edinburgh. Among the forces drawing the three together was a mutual attraction to the possibilities of steam power.

By 1761, Watt was experimenting with steam on his own, to no great avail. Then, in 1764, Watt was instructed to repair a faltering part of the school's mechanical collection: a model of John Newcomen's steam engine. His successful work on the model acquainted him intimately with not just the parts of the engine, but with its epic wastefulness of heat. That, in turn, led him to theorize that the temperature of the condensed steam should be kept as low as possible and that the cylinder should be as hot as the steam that entered it, and both realizations led him to the act of genius that would result in his breakthrough: a separate condenser where the steam could be held distinct from the main cylinder. Happily, too, metallurgy had just recently advanced to a state where boring machines could achieve the fine tolerance Watt's specifications demanded. As little as five years earlier, no one could have made the machine Watt envisioned.

James Watt left the employ of the university not long after his breakthrough. He was working in Glasgow as a civil engineer in 1768 when he completed a radical new design for a steam engine that would be three times cheaper to operate than any on the market. The following year, he secured his first patent and almost simultaneously his first patron: John Roebuck, a Scottish iron manufacturer who bought a two-thirds interest in Watt's patent. For Watt, it must have seemed like a moment of deliverance. After years of increasingly single-minded pursuit, he had finally created a steam engine worthy of market dominance, and in Roebuck, Watt had found someone who purportedly could supply what he so clearly lacked: business sense, and a capacity for the technicalities of finance and marketplace maneuvering.

In fact, the union didn't work at all. While Watt fiddled endlessly with his creation, Roebuck fumed. "You are letting the most part of your life insensibly glide away," he once wrote to his inventor. In truth, though, Roebuck didn't bring much to the table either—he lacked true money and, in the end, he lacked sense as well. An investment in a risky mining adventure drove Roebuck deeply into debt, and the economic depression of 1773 finished him off. Four years after he had entered into a partnership with the man who would help to change the global economy forever, John

Roebuck declared bankruptcy. It was the second big break for James Watt.

The third and biggest break of Watt's life came when a Birmingham businessman named Matthew Boulton, seeking to satisfy his own claims against Roebuck, picked through his slim portfolio of assets and plucked the one that no one else seemed to want: the steam-engine patent—the intellectual capital, that is, of James Watt. Partnership with Roebuck had been a marriage made, if not in hell, then in its close-in suburbs. In Boulton, though, Watt would find the perfect life's partner, and in Birmingham both would find the ideal city to turn the world on its ear.

What Florence is to the Renaissance, Birmingham arguably is to the Industrial Revolution. Almost new by English standards—the city barely existed in the time of Godric—Birmingham nonetheless had an old history in what might be thought of as an early version of heavy industry. A "goldesmythe" is known to have lived in the town in the mid-fifteenth century, and a 1538 account by the historian Leland describes it as "a good market towne...with many smithes...that use to make knives and all manner of cuttynge tools and many lorimers that make byts and a great many naylors." (Lorimers made bits and metal mountings for horses' bridles and, more generally, small iron wares. Naylors manufactured just what their name implies—iron nails.) During the English Civil War (1642–1649), the anti-royalist craftsmen, smithies, and forges of Birmingham turned out fifteen thousand sword blades for the Parliamentary forces, while declining to manufacture any for the armies of the crown.

The reason for such a predilection to metal work and machinery lies in the soil: Both iron ore and coal were locally available. Skills have a way of migrating to resources, and industry takes root where the skills and materials to serve it are in great profusion. But raw materials and industrial capacity alone don't make a revolution. To do that the new power of technology had to be wed to intellectual capacity and the raw power of ideas, and by the 1760s, Birmingham was prepared to provide those in abundance, too.

The Birmingham-based Lunar Society brought together a collection of civic boosters, captains of commerce, scientists, doctors, and out-and-out intellectuals such as the world has seldom seen. The group gathered monthly for dinner and conversation, at the time of the full moon so, weather permitting, there would be light for the walk home afterwards. (Thus the group's name, and the name by which members referred to themselves: Lunatics.) The society's meetings were devoted to discussing the great scientific and philosophical questions of the day, but this was no assemblage of dilettantes or abstract academicians. As much proto-Rotarian as they were proto-Mensa, Lunatics also meant to raise the image of Birmingham and of the products turned out there—both because they themselves stood to benefit directly in many cases and because for many of them the true test of an idea was its utility in the marketplace.

Among the Lunatics were John Baskerville, perhaps the foremost printer of his day and the creator of a singularly beautiful type face that still bears his name; Erasmus Darwin (grandfather of Charles Darwin), a scientist, poet, and among the foremost physicians of the late eighteenth century; Richard Lovell Edgeworth, a leading educational theorist whose granddaughter, Maria Edgeworth, would achieve fame for such novels as *The Absentee, Castle Rackrent,* and *Ormond;* Joseph Priestley, famous in his own time as a dissenting minister (he'd come to Birmingham to be cominister at the New Meeting Church) but more famous in history as the discoverer of oxygen; John Smeaton, who, like James Watt, started his career as a maker of mathematical instruments and who went on to found the civil engineering profession in England; and Josiah Wedgwood, the great potter. (Wedgwood's daughter, Susannah, would be the mother of Erasmus Darwin's grandson, the famous Charles.)

William Murdoch was a Lunatic, too. A leading inventor who came to Birmingham to work for Matthew Boulton and James Watt, Murdoch nearly ended up out-thinking the latter. It was Murdoch whose experiments with the distillation of coal led to the widespread use of coal gas for lighting, Murdoch who perfected the compression of air to make a functioning steam gun, and Murdoch who, as we'll later see, might have led Boulton and Watt to even greater triumphs had they only listened to him.

Others in the group included Sir John Whitehurst, perhaps the most famous clock maker of his time in England, and the physician William Withering, whom Erasmus Darwin asked to join after his own doctor and fellow original member William Small died. (Small himself had been a friend of Benjamin Franklin.) Seeking to cure what appeared to be a fatally ill patient, Withering pursued a familiar gypsy remedy for heart disease—the foxglove plant—and thus discovered digitalis, which remains the most widely used drug for the treatment of the condition. By most accounts, he also became the richest physician in England working outside of London. Though he was never more than transient in Birmingham, Sir William Herschel was a Lunatic as well, and among the most distinguished of them all. German born, he'd come to Bath in the mid-1760s to work as an organist and ended up the best known astronomer of his time. Herschel founded sidereal astronomy; he was the first to theorize that Mars had icecaps marked by polar snow, much like Earth; and for good measure, he discovered the planet Uranus, using a telescope laughable by today's standards.

And then there was Matthew Boulton. An entrepreneur and industrialist, he was perhaps among the least accomplished members of the Lunar Society, at least as judged by intellectual output. He was also absolutely central to the group: He and Erasmus Darwin had been the founders, and the group met over dinner at his spacious home, Soho House. Because Boulton manufactured everything from buttons to buckles, coins, and fancy ornamentation, he also had the most to gain by elevating the image of Birmingham and its products.

Like other Lunatics, Matthew Boulton appears to have been unable to resist innovation. Set on three hundred acres of landscaped parkland, his neoclassical mansion was thought to be the most technologically advanced house in England by the end of the eighteenth century. A central heating system, almost unheard of since the Roman legions retreated from Great Britain, used a network of ducts to distribute hot air from a cellar furnace—small holes even warmed the stairs. As late as 1995, when the mansion (now reduced to one acre) was being restored by the Birmingham City Council, the furnace was still in working order. Outside, Boulton used a novel slate siding covered with paint and sand to preserve a uniform appearance to the mansion even as he added wing after wing. To fill the dimples made by the hammer where it secured the slates, Boulton used buttons from his factory. He even experimented with alloy window frames, and he was also a cook, fond of serving the Lunatics a hearty dish called "Birmingham Soup." (The directions call for, among other ingredients, "one leg of beef.")

The endless improving, the love of innovation almost for its own sake, the house filled with geegaws, even the attention to food, call to mind Thomas Jefferson at Monticello, his mountainside home just south of Charlottesville, Virginia. Indeed there was much in the spirit of the times that appealed to forward-thinking visionaries on both sides of the ocean. Among Lunar Society members, Joseph Priestley fiercely advocated the colonies' side and would spend the last decade of his life in America, where his sons had already settled. But whereas Jefferson clung to something close to the agrarian ideal—the nobility of those who work the soil—Matthew Boulton believed in the nobility of machines. He liked to make things, almost anything. And he had the factory to do it.

A maker of commercial buttons at the start of his career—and the beneficiary of several financially providential marriages—Boulton was running almost a conglomerate by the time he met James Watt. Not one to shy away from high-end items, and not cowed by the difficulty of doing business abroad, Boulton had been in the ormolu business from mid-century, turning out highly ornamented, imitation-gold clock cases for sale domestically and on the continent. He moved into the silver trade as well, hiring some of the best known artists of his day to do designs, including Robert Adam. For his fellow Lunatic Josiah Wedgwood, Boulton's factory manufactured the metal frames for Wedgwood cameos. (Wedgwood, in turn, would describe Boulton in 1769 as the "first manufacturer in England.") Sword hilts, shoe buckles, and watch fobs also poured from Boulton's works—whatever forms metal could take for profit, it seemed, including coins. It was with his minting business in mind that Boulton once lamented to the Lords of the Privy Council that, "The public has sustained great loss by the illegal practice of counterfeiting halfpence which has lately been carried to a great height than was ever before known and seems still to increase." Nor did Boulton shy away from promoting his wares. There's more than a hint of a modern direct-mail campaign in the printed letters Boulton blanketed the countryside with in advance of a 1771 auction of his goods.

By the time he secured the rights to James Watt's first steam engine patent in the mid-1770s, Matthew Boulton owned the biggest and most modern manufacturing plant in Britain. The plant, known as the Soho Manufactory, used dozens of machines and employed six hundred workers, in conditions that powerfully presaged the world to come. Boulton's many products moved down assembly lines, forbearers of the ones Henry Ford's Model Ts would move down a century and a quarter later. To retain and protect his most skilled workers, Boulton also provided an early form of medical insurance. Little wonder both man and factory became so famous in their day. Boulton's Manufactory attracted so many visitors that he had to schedule guided tours, and he liked to use the tours to further enhance his reputation and promote his products. When Samuel Johnson arrived in 1774 for a look at the works, Boulton commented to the famous literary czar: "I sell here, Sir, what all the world desires to have—power." Even taken metaphorically, it was no idle boast. Matthew Boulton stood at the center of industrial Birmingham, and Birmingham stood at the center of the industrial world.

James Watt would give Boulton yet another product line, what was to become his best one of all. Almost no sooner had he secured the rights to Watt's patent than Boulton formed a new enterprise—Boulton & Watt—to produce the engine. At Boulton's urging (and arguably solely because of his urging) the methodical Watt completed a working engine in only five months, just as the coal industry in England was reaching a crisis point. The further into the earth men dug for coal, the more underground springs they tapped, and the greater the expense of keeping both the men and work areas dry. Newcomen's steam-driven mine pumps used so much fuel that they were driving mine owners to abandon their holdings. Watt's engine offered an economical alternative that helped rescue an entire industry. As product and need merged, the coal business turned around, and as that happened, Boulton & Watt began selling steam-driven pumps as fast as it could turn them out. By 1783, the two men had cornered the market in Cornwall, home of

England's richest coal mines. Boulton & Watt's engine required only a quarter as much fuel as Newcomen's had; in return, the firm took one-third of the savings. For years James Watt had lived on the edge of poverty in Glasgow. Now, suddenly, he was rich.

For his part, Boulton gave Watt what John Roebuck had only promised to give: real business savvy, an entrepreneur's instinct for opportunity and promotion, some of the deepest pockets in England, and a pleasing public face. Watt once described himself as "out of my sphere when I have anything to do with mankind." The buoyant Boulton, by contrast, seems almost always to have been involved with mankind. While Boulton saw to the day-to-day matters, Watt could fiddle with his engine in private, and fiddle he still needed to do. Boulton & Watt had cornered the mining market to be sure, but neither the firm nor its inventive genius had solved the fundamental problem of powering the Industrial Revolution.

James Watt's engine was reciprocating: It moved up and down, and only up and down. For all its refinements, the engine was still a pump, capable of doing only the things a pump can do—and removing water from mines was perhaps the most profitable of those things in late eighteenth century England. Matthew Boulton wanted a rotary engine, one that could turn things. Until then, even his great Manufactory would have to continue depending on running water and waterwheels.

❦

If the history of James Watt and the stream engine is relatively clear up to the moment his smart steam-powered pump became a smart engine, the record tends to cloud over at the actual moment of translation. Patent applications, which might in other circumstances help clarify the sequence of events, instead have the opposite effect. In an age rife with industrial espionage and patent litigation, specifications were written broadly enough to discourage imitators and obscurely enough to be all-inconclusive. ("I cannot pretend to say what ingenious vagaries engineers might run into after reading B&W's specifications," a rival wrote of one of Boulton & Watt steam-engine patent applications. "Perhaps they would have a nice and warm water closet.")

Certainly, Boulton pushed Watt to make the leap from reciprocation to rotation; always open to new ideas, Boulton couldn't have stopped himself if he wanted to. Certainly, Watt kept on inventing—he couldn't have stopped that either. And certainly, the critical changes got made, beginning with the "sun-and-planet" gearing system that translated Watt's up-and-down engine motion into a rotary one. What is unknown is the role of William Murdoch in the great translation. Murdoch was as much an inventor as Watt—a millwright's son, he walked two hundred and fifty miles to Birmingham in 1777 just to land a job with Soho Manufactory—and he could be every bit as annoying as Watt, too, with his own tinkering and incessant questioning. (Watt once complained of Murdoch in a letter that he "always said when anything was proposed to be done, however well contrived, 'ay, but there is another way of doing it' "—a case, perhaps, of the pot calling the kettle black.) But Watt and Boulton were owners; Murdoch, though admitted to the Lunar Society, was only a worker; and in practical terms, it really doesn't matter all that much.

With a rotary engine, Boulton could power his own machinery independently of running water—his mint, most especially—and what Soho Manufactory could do, others quickly aspired to do as well. Soon, Boulton & Watt engines were powering iron foundries, other manufacturing plants, and the critical textile industry all across England. The country, Boulton once said, was "steam mill mad." A small island nation was on its way to becoming the strongest economic power in the world, and Matthew Boulton and James Watt were riding the crest of wealth and fame. By the start of the new nineteenth century, it wasn't just literary lords who were calling on Boulton, but literal lords and ladies from all over Europe. When Lord Nelson, the naval commander and greatest national hero of his time, visited Birmingham in 1802, Soho House was his first stop.

The two founders retired from Boulton & Watt in 1800— good friends and two of the richest men in England—and turned the business over to their sons. Not surprisingly, for Watt retirement was just a continuation of what he had always done. In his later years, he patented a machine for drawing perspectives, a letter-copying process, and a steam wheel that he had hoped would produce rotary motion directly from steam power, without the intervening gear system. (He never completed the work.) One of Watt's last inventions, at age 83, was a machine for copying sculptures. Boulton, for his part, kept welcoming the grand and the curious to his estate and the factory he had begun so many years earlier. Glad-handing was another of his many skills. Watt died at his estate outside Birmingham in 1819, at age 83; Boulton had died on his own estate 10 years earlier, just shy of his 81st birthday.

⤳

Who was the greater of the two friends? History has already cast that vote, resoundingly. The *Dictionary of Scientific Biography*, published under the auspices of the American Council of Learned Societies and edited by a blue-ribbon panel of academicians, barely mentions Boulton in its entry on Watt. The *Encyclopedia Britannica* devotes less than half a column to its entry on Boulton, while it lavishes two columns on Watt. Watt is also the subject of numerous children's science books meant to inspire young minds. To some degree history is right. All great new inventions and applications begin with great new ideas.

Sir Nicholas Goodison, the former chairman of London's International Stock Exchange and the author of a book-length study of Boulton and his output, disagrees. "It's typical of Britain and British culture to glorify Watt the inventor and not Boulton the entrepreneur," he told *Institutional Investor* magazine. Without getting into the subtleties of British culture, Goodison has a point, too. Even a great idea is only an idea until someone comes along with the practical skills to turn it into a product and to acquaint the world with its uses. For James Watt, that person was Matthew Boulton.

But maybe the larger point is that history was never right to separate the two men in the first place. Like the company they founded, Boulton & Watt should always be joined by an ampersand. Without the entrepreneurial Boulton to bring buzz and energy and a broader vision of how the technology should be applied, James Watt had on his hands a really terrific method for getting water out of deep holes—hardly the stuff of history. It was Boulton who pushed Watt forward, who drove him to consider how to turn reciprocation into rotation, and who forced him to stop theorizing and start realizing. Unable to temper Watt's in-born pessimism, Boulton lent him his own optimism when it most counted. Thus, the argument for Boulton. Yet without the inventive Watt to take an existing technology and move it a quantum leap forward, Matthew Boulton had no ultimate product to apply his entrepreneurial and business skills to. He was a zealot in search of a cause. What was most maddening in Watt—his epic single-mindedness and grinding persistence—was also what was most invaluable, and much as he wanted product, Boulton had the native sense to understand that. As partnerships go, theirs was a model of success. Divided, they might have stood just fine; united, they helped change the world, although not quite as thoroughly as they might have.

It was in 1784 that Boulton apparently first suggested Watt develop a steam engine capable of powering a moving carriage. William Murdoch, the silent partner in the Soho Manufactory, would take the suggestion to heart: Murdoch "has mentioned to me a new scheme which you may be assured he is very intent upon, but which he is afraid of mentioning to you for fear of your laughing at him," Boulton wrote to Watt. "It is no less than drawing carriages upon the road with steam engines." As it turned out, Boulton, like any great leader, knew his players well: Murdoch did go on to build a working miniature of his engine, and Watt dismissed the whole business out of hand, telling his partner that he held "small hopes that a wheel carriage would ever become useful."

The steam engine that would power the first locomotive would radically alter transportation across England and throughout Europe. Across the ocean, it would even pull a continent together. But its invention and manufacture would be left to other minds and hands.

6

THE TRANSCONTINENTAL RAILROAD

Rogues and Visionaries

ICTURE, FOR A MOMENT, A MAP OF THE UNITED States in 1860. Civil war is about to transform the nation you are looking at. Nearly half a million Americans on both sides of the conflict will be killed, either in combat or at its fringes. About one in every sixty people alive at the start of the war will be dead at the end of it. But if tragedy waits in the wings, the map itself should look very familiar. America's contiguous borders have remained the same ever since the Gadsden Purchase of 1853. The last great territorial addition, the purchase of Alaska from Russia, is only seven years in the future.

Not only has the outline of the nation been fixed; from the East Coast to the Mississippi River, America is beginning to grow in population and fill itself. Boston has been around for almost two and a half centuries, and Philadelphia for nearly as long. By the mid-1680s, Philadelphia contained about six hundred houses, many of them brick; almost a century later, when the Continental Congress met there, the population stood at forty thousand people. To the South, the Charleston of 1860 boasts perhaps the nation's most cosmopolitan assemblage, including America's largest Jewish community. A late starter among major urban centers, New York City is roaring ahead of everyone else. In 1850, it had finally crossed the half-million mark in residents; now, it seems there's no stopping the place. Chicago has only thirty thousand residents, but its location at the foot of Lake Michigan makes it the nation's largest railroad center. Eleven states—Illinois, Indiana, Kentucky, and Missouri, among them—all have more than a million residents. Slavery and states' rights issues are splitting the country, but at least they are forcing Americans to think about their own nationhood and what it means.

Life is bustling on the other side of the continent, too. In July 1850, five hundred ghost ships had crowded San Francisco Bay, all of them deserted by their sailors in favor of the inland streams lined—so legend had it—with gold. By 1860, the gold rush is over, but the prospectors and the businessmen who profited from them linger on. The census of 1850 had counted 92,597 people living in California; by 1860, that number has swelled more than four-fold, to nearly 380,000. By the start of the Civil War, San Francisco already boasts newspapers, magazines, theaters, and libraries. Back east, the city has gained a reputation for something approaching sophistication, if only one could get there. And therein lies the problem.

Maps of the time show an Eastern United States nearing adulthood and a West Coast rippling with new energy separated by—both nothing and everything. Cartographers of the time commonly referred to the vast stretch between the Mississippi River and the California mountains as the Great American Desert. The most spectacular part of it, the Grand Canyon, they didn't bother to map at all: Until a one-armed Civil War vet named John Wesley Powell undertook a death-defying run through the canyon on the Colorado River in August 1869, no European-American had ever tried even to define its boundaries.

It wasn't that transportation technology was lacking; the problem was distance and a forbidding terrain. By 1829,

Englishman George Stephenson's Rocket had shown that a steam-propelled locomotive could provide reliable, high-volume transportation at a low enough cost to make it economically feasible for people and products. Suddenly, the Industrial Revolution had wheels and rolling stock. The first steam-locomotive built for regular duty in the United States went into service in Charleston in 1830. Thirty years later, a spider web of thirty thousand miles of track crisscrossed the East clear to the Mississippi and in some rare cases beyond it. The Chicago and Rock Island railroad, which had linked Chicago to the Mississippi in 1854, was the first to build a rail bridge across that river. Downstream, a locomotive that was to become part of the Missouri Pacific line had made a five-mile foray west of St. Louis as early as 1852. By 1859, the Hannibal and St. Joseph Railroad had reached the Missouri River. But that was as far as even the pioneer rails went. Ahead lay nearly two thousand miles of plains, scorching desert, and towering mountains cut by deep canyons, and protected by native Americans ready to take a last stand against the loss of their tribal lands.

Lead the iron horse across that majestic, terrifying expanse, and you would connect the two economic loci of America and create a powerhouse such as the world had never seen. The great American breadbasket was waiting to be planted; the Rockies harbored one of the world's great mineral reserves. Horse-drawn wagons could cross from one side of the country to the other, and ships could carry goods and passengers around Cape Horn, or from ocean to ocean via a land portage across Nicaragua or Panama. But wagons lacked volume, and both modes of transportation were too slow. Only trains could carry in settlers and supplies, and carry out grain, silver, timber, oil, and more. Bring East and West together, and market would feed market and spawn new markets as surely as day follows dawn. What was needed wasn't engines. What was needed was track, and people with the will and gumption to lay it.

⤸

The Transcontinental Railroad was the Apollo Project of the nineteenth century—one of those rare moments in history when discovery and technology seems to be colliding with destiny. National pride was at stake, and national aspiration, and something bigger still: Just as the manned landing on the moon would do, the railroad conquered an unknown world, planted a first tentative foot in an unknown space. Only those present could see the final spike of iron, clad in silver and gold, being driven into the last link of rail at Promontory Summit, Utah, on May 10, 1869, but the event was broadcast by telegraph and followed by Americans as avidly—and greeted as enthusiastically—as Neil Armstrong's lunar "giant step for mankind" almost exactly one hundred years later, on July 20, 1969.

Getting the two rail lines to Promontory Summit had involved six years and $200 million dollars—more than 10 percent of all the money the federal government took in during those years, and this despite huge outlays for the final years of the Civil War. Thousands of men had worked in sometimes deplorable conditions across a perilous landscape, and more than one hundred of them had perished in the effort. Yet despite the rigor, even at times the horror, of the enterprise, contemporary dispatches make its final moments seem almost like a ballet:

"At 2:20 this afternoon, Washington time, all the telegraph offices in the country were notified by the Omaha telegraph office to be ready to receive the signals corresponding to the blows of the hammer that drove the last spike in the last rail that united New York and San Francisco with a band of iron," the Washington *Evening Star* reported on the front page of its May 10, 1869, edition.

Accordingly Mr. Tinker, Manager of the W.U. telegraph office in this city, placed a magnetic bell-sounder in the public office of that company, corner 14th street and [Pennsylvania] avenue, connected the same with the main lines, and notified the various offices that he was ready. New Orleans instantly responded, the answer being read from the bell-taps, 'that he was ready.' New York did the same. At 2:27 offices over the country began to make all sorts of inquiries of Omaha, to which that office replied: '*To Everybody:* Keep quiet. When the last spike is driven at Promontory Point, they will say "done." Don't break the circuit, but watch for the signals of the blows of the hammer.'

Just as Omaha was hushing the rest of the nation, the Promontory Summit telegraph office began to weigh in with its own blow by blow of the events, according to the *Evening Star* account:

"Almost ready," the word came from Utah, "Hats off. Prayer is being offered." A silence for the prayer ensued. At 2:40 the bell tapped again, and the office at the Point said: "We have got done praying. The spike is about to be presented."

Chicago replied, "We understand. All are ready in the East."

Promontory Point: "All ready now. The spike will be driven. The signal will be three dots for the commencement of the blows." For a moment the instrument was silent, then the hammer of the magnet tapped the bell—one-two-three—the signal! Another pause for a few seconds, and the lightning came flashing Eastward, vibrating over twenty-four hundred miles between the junction of the two roads and Washington—and the blows of the hammer upon the spike were measured instantly in telegraphic accents on the bell here. At 2:47 pm, Promontory Point gave the signal, "done," and the continent was spanned with iron!

In New York—the *Times* of May 11, 1869, reported—the driving of the final spike was met with the "booming of cannon, peals from Trinity chimes, and general rejoicing over the completion of the great enterprise, in the success of which not only this country, but the whole civilized world, is directly interested." Philadelphia marked the historic moment by tolling the bells of Independence Hall, where the nation had begun. Although undermanned in population, Chicagoans spontaneously formed a parade line said to be seven miles in length. In California, anxious celebrants ignored some last minute delays in completing the track and went on with the planned festivities. In San Francisco what was supposed to have been a "done" signal snaked along a telegraph wire that had been laid under the city streets out to Fort Point, where it detonated a 15-inch cannon. In Sacramento, 23 Central Pacific locomotives let loose with their whistles for a good 15 minutes, at the time the last spike was scheduled to have been driven in back in Utah.

At Promontory Summit itself, the work of driving the final gold-clad spike—with a ceremonial silver hammer—was done by representatives of the two railroads that had done all the work. The Central Pacific Railroad, which had laid the track east from Sacramento across the Sierra Nevadas and into the Rocky Mountains, was represented along the south track by its president, Leland Stanford, who doubled at the time as governor of California. Along the north track stood Dr. Thomas C. Durant, vice president of and the driving force behind the Union Pacific, which had laid the track west more than a thousand miles from Omaha, Nebraska. Only days earlier, "Doc" Durant—he liked the appellation even though he hadn't practiced opthamology in decades—had been taken hostage by his own workers, or so the story went.

110

At the signal "O.K." from the telegraph office, Stanford took a whack, Durant finished off the job, and the Atlantic and Pacific oceans were joined across the continent by rail for the first time. Soon thereafter, Grenville M. Dodge, the chief engineer of the project on the Union Pacific side, wired Secretary of War General John A. Rawlins from Promontory Summit that, "... today the last rail was laid at this point. 1,086 miles from Missouri River and 690 miles from Sacramento. The great work, commenced during the Administration of LINCOLN, in the middle of a great rebellion, is completed under that of GRANT, who conquered the peace."

Later in the day back in Washington, D.C., the *Evening Star* editorialized for its readers that "Today, May 10th, 1869, witnesses an event which must pass into history as one of the most important of the century, as well in respect to its immediate as its future effects upon this country and the human race."

"It only remains for us to congratulate the enterprising and liberal spirits who conceived and executed a work at once so useful and so great, and the country which is to enjoy its golden and perennial fruits," the editorial concluded. "A more pleasant duty we have rarely had to perform."

If only, in fact, it had been that simple. Historic, yes—and beyond doubt one of the most important achievements of the century, for America and the world. But when it came to the principals involved, the *Evening Star* sugar-coated the story almost to the point of non-recognition. Behind the railroad and its completion lay a rogue's gallery of colorful characters. Audacious tasks, it turns out, require audacious people, and the Transcontinental Railroad would bring them out in droves.

The story of the Transcontinental Railroad begins with geography and ends in greed and profit. By the mid-nineteenth century America was a divided country politically: Climate, the nature of the soil, immigration patterns, economic interests, slavery and much more had driven a wide wedge between

North and South. But the United States was a country divided by its own vastness as well. East of the Mississippi was a nation that had grown up largely under English tutelage. On the West Coast sat a second America, born under Spanish rule and only now being anglicized, in large part by the influence of the prospectors and other easterners who had rushed to California during the 1849 gold craze. Until the space between the regions could be closed and settled, the United States was united in name only, whatever the resolution of the political schism might be.

Crossing and closing that larger continental divide would make a handful of men immensely rich, and riches are what got them into the project in the first place. But before there was greed, there was idealism. Visionary nationalists like Asa Whitney had been urging a transcontinental railroad since the 1840s, almost from the moment that the great age of the American railroad was born. Egged on by Whitney and others, Congress had been debating the subject for two decades before the first piece of transcontinental track was ever laid down.

The hard rock that the railroad idealists kept running up against was politics. Northern interests envisioned a route that began in Chicago—as most convenient to the industrial and population centers of the northeast—and headed west through the Dakotas. Southern interests wanted Atlanta to be the eastern terminus of a line that would follow the trail eventually blazed by the Atchison, Topeka, and Santa Fe. A central route backed by the powerful Missouri Senator Thomas Hart Benton, great-uncle to the famous artist of the same name, would take off for the west from Omaha, running along Nebraska's Platte River Valley.

By 1862, when a package of federal loans to fund the Transcontinental Railroad finally cleared Congress, the choice had been simplified—the secessionist South no longer had a say or a vote in the matter. The Civil War gave a boost to the project in another way, just as the Cold War a century later would provide a rationale for funding the Interstate Highway system: Rather than just serve the purposes of settlement and commerce, the Transcontinental Railroad was now essential for the national defense, to assure the easy movement of troops and supplies. Presented with the funding and asked to choose among the remaining possible routes, Abraham Lincoln sided with Benton and his central route, and the railroad was ready to begin its westward march. (Lincoln, who owned several pieces of real estate in Council Bluffs, Iowa, across the Missouri from Omaha, was careful to acknowledge his own self-interest in the selection.)

By then, too, the greatest impediment to the eastward movement of the railroad out of Sacramento had been solved by another of the Transcontinental's dreamers, as opposed to its schemers. Born in Connecticut and trained as a civil engineer in New York before migrating to California, Theodore Judah had set himself the monumental task of finding a practical way to move tracks and trains out of the Sacramento Valley, up the Sierra Nevadas, and back down again into Nevada and Utah beyond. For month upon month, Judah trekked through the High Sierras until he found the perfect solution in perhaps the most infamous terrain in all of the mountain range: Donner Pass, where during the brutal winter of 1846–1847, a group of settlers had fallen victim to starvation and cannibalism while trying to reach California.

Soon thereafter, Theodore Judah would mention both his route and the use he foresaw for it during a chance encounter with Collis Huntington, and with that, anything that remotely resembled idealism would pretty much disappear from the picture.

Also Connecticut-born and New York–raised, Collis Huntington had a genius for making money. A pushcart salesman in his youth, he'd come west with the Gold Rush, but instead of digging and panning for gold, he ended up selling prospectors the shovels and picks they needed to do the work, a far more certain source of profit. By 1861, Huntington was running a prosperous hardware company in Sacramento, with Mark Hopkins. Then Theodore Judah wandered into the store, and Collis Huntington knew he was staring opportunity in the face.

He and Hopkins recruited two other partners: Leland Stanford, who had failed as a lawyer back East and was in partnership with his brothers a few blocks away in the wholesale grocery business, and Charles Crocker, who had come west in 1849 to find gold and, failing that, had set himself up as a drygoods merchant, also in Sacramento. Together, the four men put up $24,000 to form the Central Pacific Railroad corporation and began their ride to fortune—and what a ride it would be.

Collis Huntington's fortune eventually would grow to something on the order of $70 million, built not just on trains, but on timber, coal mines, steamship lines, and Southern California real estate as well. Rail, though, remained his fortune's fount and his own first love. By the mid-1890s Huntington was able to travel entirely on track he owned from his mansion on San Francisco's Nob Hill to Newport News, Virginia, which he had founded as the deep-water terminus for another of his investments, the Chesapeake & Ohio Railroad. Near the end of his life, he bought a summer camp in New York's Adirondack mountains and had a 26-mile railroad spur built so that the camp would be easier to reach from a Fifth Avenue mansion he also owned in Manhattan. In time, his heirs would use the fortune to fund the renowned Huntington Library in San Marino, California.

Huntington's original partner, Mark Hopkins, was the first of the four to die, in 1878, but not before he and his wife also built a mansion on Nob Hill—with a drawing room modeled

St. Godric was one of a relative handful of capitalist pioneers who escaped the agrarian life—depicted here in a Flemish painting of farmers making hay—and helped launch the millennium of business.

In this painting of Dante holding the *Divine Comedy*, the poet stands with purgatory on his left and the Cathedral of Florence on his right. In real life, the great Florentine banker and patron of the arts Cosimo de' Medici had to find a middle ground between the sin of usury and the personal wealth that helped make Florence the birthplace of the Renaissance.

In this depiction of Toledo, El Greco's dramatic chiaro-
scuro foreshadows the dark times Spain would face under
the artist's patron, Philip II.

At the height
of Tulipmania,
one Viceroy
bulb was worth
eight pigs, four
oxen, 24 tons
of wheat, 10
tons of butter,
and a thousand
pounds of
cheese.

James Watt's steam engine might never have gone into production had the Scottish inventor not met the English entrepreneur and manufacturer Matthew Boulton. Together, though, the two unlocked the potential in Watt's inventive genius and launched the Industrial Revolution.

On April 10, 1869, the government announced that the Union Pacific and Central Pacific railroads would meet at Promontory Summit, Utah. With an end point finally in sight, crews began to work around the clock to lay the last 100 miles of track.

J.P. Morgan single-handedly rescued Wall Street from the 1907 crisis that caused this rush on a bank. Wary of the fact that one man possessed such tremendous power, the government soon created the Federal Reserve system.

Ruthless in business but generous in philanthropy, John D. Rockefeller was "a man of relentless contradictions, all of which he carried to an absolute extreme."

Americans bought 10,000 Model Ts in 1908, its first year of production, as Henry Ford set out to democratize the automobile. Nineteen years later, when Ford finally replaced the Model T with the Model A and had to turn to advertising to move his product, he was heard to grumble: "We are no longer in the automobile business."

Robert Woodruff, pictured here, capitalized on the Consumer Revolution, making Coca-Cola a worldwide brand associated with patriotism, wholesome values, and the essence of America itself.

The Warner brothers had a vision long before they had the means to fulfill it: When they lacked the money to hire Charlie Chaplin, they compromised by hiring his brother, Sydney, shown here in an early poster.

Famously contentious, Bill Gates is also a philanthropist and visionary. He is shown here shaking hands with Boston schoolchildren, after donating $100,000 to an after-school program that gives inner-city students access to computers.

on a chamber of the Palace of the Doges, a dining room capable of seating sixty, and a master bedroom done up in ebony with ivory inlay. Today, the Mark Hopkins Hotel has appropriated his name and sits on that site.

Another Nob Hill resident, Leland Stanford—his and Hopkins' mansions sat side by side—would leave more lasting legacies. Stanford became the chief financial backer of the California Street Cable Railway (parent to the cable cars that still amuse San Francisco tourists) in the 1870s. He also served eight years in the U.S. Senate, until his death in 1893, and of course he founded the university that bears the name of his son—dead at age 15—and that has helped, at least in part, to polish a reputation not notable in its time for generous public acts. (In his charming history of the Central Pacific's founders, *Big Four*, Oscar Lewis notes that in 1894 Arthur McEwen had suggested that the arch above the entrance to Stanford University should read: "With Apologies to God.")

Charles Crocker also built a mansion on Nob Hill—this one of redwood, at a cost of $1.25 million, with a 76-foot tower for the views. Like Huntington, he also would spread his interests into coal, banking, local real estate, and irrigation development in the San Joaquin Valley. Like all the partners, too, he was part of a world that freely flowed between commerce and government: Crocker's brother served as chief justice of the California Supreme Court during Leland Stanford's term as governor. But Charles Crocker more than any of the others had been involved in the day-to-day management of the Central Pacific in its early years, and he never stopped keeping a close eye on the enterprise. Always overweight and subject to medical problems, he went into a diabetic coma in August 1888 and died at the new resort hotel at Del Monte that the railroad had only recently completed at his urging. His estate was said to be worth $40 million.

Getting so rich, though, would take both time and work. Spurned by the money interests in the city they would eventually lord it over—San Francisco—and rebuffed by the legislature of the state Leland Stanford would soon govern—California—the new Central Pacific partners laid siege to the one place most capable of providing the millions of dollars they needed to begin laying rail toward the East: the United States Congress. And in the Washington of 1862, they were well-equipped for the challenge. All four had had a hand in launching the Republican Party in 1856, after the collapse of the Whig movement; and Hopkins, Stanford, and Crocker each had stood for either local or state office under the party's banner in its first years. In 1860, only four years after the party was founded, Republicans had managed to elect their first president, Abraham Lincoln. Born in abolitionist sentiment, the Republican Party also fit the spirit of the moment, at least until the war seemed to be going badly for the Union side. And in Theodore Judah, the Central Pacific crowd had not only a bold thinker but a man who brought an engineer's thoroughness to the business of lobbying.

With the help of Aaron Sargent, a newly minted California congressman with long ties to Huntington, Judah was appointed secretary of the Senate committee that was considering the Railroad Act. Soon he added, via a clerkship on the relevant House subcommittee, the position of clerk of the main House committee charged with the bill, and by then he was, in effect, writing large chunks of the legislation he was advocating. The debate that ensued was long and the opposition strong—even despite the national defense imperative and the voluntary removal of the southern-route proponents—but on July 1, 1862, President Lincoln signed the act, designating the Central Pacific to begin building the Transcontinental Railroad east from Sacramento and the Union Pacific to start building west from Omaha. Both corporations were granted what were to prove highly valuable rights of way from the federal lands they would pass through, and both were given access to government loans, payable over 30 years at 6 percent interest, for up to $48,000 per mile of track laid, depending on the terrain.

"We have drawn the elephant," Theodore Judah wired back to San Francisco as soon as the act was signed. "Now let us see if we can harness him up."

That task, though, would fall largely to others. Judah was on his way back to the East Coast from San Francisco in October 1863, sailing on the steamer *St. Louis*, when he contracted yellow fever during a land crossing in Panama. A little less than two weeks later he was dead, still short of his 38th birthday. At least he wouldn't live to witness the rapaciousness of the men who completed the job he had helped to start.

⁓

What Collis Huntington was to the Central Pacific Railroad— its dynamo, the one who traveled the length and breadth of the East, making arrangements with the foundries for more rail, staving off the bankers when the funding got perilous as it frequently did in those early years, buttonholing congressmen for more loans, and bribing them when all else failed—Thomas C. Durant was to the Union Pacific.

He had lobbied as hard as the Central Pacific had for the franchise to lay rail west from Omaha, and like the Central Pacific, he had papered Congress with favors. (Free rail travel seems to have been standard issue for congressmen in those days, and many of them—such as the powerful Pennsylvania senator Thaddeus Stevens, who owned an iron foundry—had a vested interest in the outcome in any event.) But whereas Huntington and his group appear to have had some vestiges of conscience, or at least a trace of concern about how history might view them, Durant was largely untroubled on both scores.

Officially, he held the title of vice president of the Union Pacific, but anyone in or out of the company knew that he *was* the Union Pacific. To the men who worked for him, Durant was a tyrant. His style of management, it's said, consisted largely of issuing a constant barrage of directives, most of them insulting, and often demanding that something be done immediately that could barely be done at all. When he couldn't pay his workers—and he often couldn't, or wouldn't—he would bully them to keep at the job. When they balked at that, he'd threaten to replace them on the spot.

To himself, though, Thomas Durant was the soul of generosity, and nowhere more so than in the matter of the Crédit Mobilier of America. Having secured the right to lay the rail, Durant set up Crédit Mobilier—he borrowed the better part of the name from a French corporation—as an independent construction company and then subcontracted the entire job out to his creation, which in turn charged Union Pacific outrageous rates for the work it was performing.

Like Collis Huntington, who went to bed many nights in the mid- and late 1860s wondering where the Central Pacific would find the next million dollars to meet its debts, Thomas Durant went to bed many nights aware that the Union Pacific was all but bankrupt. Durant, though, was the one who was helping to bankrupt his company, and the Crédit Mobilier gave him an added advantage: When the going got tough, he could sprinkle heavily discounted shares in his creation over Congress in lieu of hard cash. Whatever the financial health of the Union Pacific, it was no secret that Crédit Mobilier was going great guns.

And still the work got done. More than fifteen months elapsed after Abraham Lincoln signed the Railroad Act before the Central Pacific laid its first section of rail—surveying had to be completed, crews and managers brought on board, and the rail secured and brought in place. Another two years would pass before the company had laid its first 55 miles of track. Theodore Judah's route was the right one, but it still meant blasting tunnels and creating rail beds through the unyielding, unforgiving rock of the Sierra Nevadas.

Labor was a problem as well. What able-bodied men California had could generally make far better wages working in the mines and elsewhere. To fill the ranks, the Central Pacific turned to China, ultimately importing some twelve thousand workers from Canton province. The men—more than half were, in fact, teenagers—earned $30 a month laying rail. For much of the time, they camped alongside the track as they went, no easy chore in the dead of winter.

"When the snow got so bad, usually they would live beneath [it]," David Haward Bain, author of *Empire Express*, told television interviewer Brian Lamb. "They would just carve out entire galleries underneath the snow and live there for months at a time."

Amazingly, they were well provided for, Stephen Ambrose writes in his history of the Transcontinental Railroad, *Nothing Like It in the World*. The Cantonese dined on oysters, cuttlefish, bamboo sprouts, seaweed, mushrooms, and many other delicacies reminiscent of the homes and farms they had left—all dried and sent out from Chinese merchants in San Francisco. Unlike their American-born counterparts, the Cantonese also bathed regularly, and although they smoked opium on Sundays, they mostly stayed away from alcohol. The white worker "has a sort of hydrophobia which induces him to avoid the contact of water," one observer of the work gangs noted, whereas "the Chinaman is accustomed to daily ablution of his entire person."

Working out from the western edge of the settled nation, the Union Pacific had a larger labor pool to draw from. Irish immigrants did much of the early work, joined by hardened veterans as the Civil War drew to a close. Until they reached the Rockies, the Union Pacific workers did not encounter the challenging terrain of their competitors—they laid rail far faster, at far less revenue per mile—but they paid for the flatter land in parching summer temperatures, bitter winter winds, and vulnerability to Indian attacks. None of the mileage, on either side, came easy.

By 1866, the two railroads collectively were the biggest employers in the United States, with twenty thousand men on their payrolls. By mid-1868, the Union Pacific had crossed the Rockies and was racing across Wyoming. In April, the company had laid track across Sherman Summit: At 8,242 feet, it would be the highest elevation either company conquered in the building of the Transcontinental Railroad. Not long after, Union Pacific took the railroad across the Dale Creek chasm with a 700-foot-long bridge built of wood, 126 feet above the stream bed, one of the great engineering feats of the century and done almost on the fly.

To the west in Nevada, Charles Crocker had vowed that his crews would lay a mile of track a day during 1868, and they almost made it, falling only three miles short. By now, the workers were living in boxcars that rolled along with the railhead. At stake for both railroads was the lion's share of the rail traffic in Brigham Young's prosperous Mormon community in Utah, which was expected to swell with European settlers once the railroad was open. To hedge the Central Pacific's bet, Leland Stanford spent much of the fall and winter in Salt Lake City courting Young. As 1869 dawned, they were addressing each other as "Brigham" and "Leland."

On April 10, 1869, the government finally set a meeting point for the two companies: a desolate spot in the Utah mountains called Promontory Summit, six miles west of Ogden. With more than sixteen hundred miles and some six years of labor behind them and only a collective one hundred miles left to go, men began to work around the clock, performing what seem, in retrospect, astounding feats: Even with dynamiting through rock to make the beds, crews were laying ten miles of track in a single day. Not everything got done right—the Central Pacific crew left some weird z-shaped tracks behind them for later railroad crews and railroad barons to worry about— but the job did get done. America was too anxious to be joined coast to coast to dawdle.

May 10, 1869—a month to the day after the meeting point had been set—broke clear in Promontory Summit, and cold enough that the one watery street in town was frozen solid. Leland Stanford and Mark Hopkins were there to represent the Central Pacific. (According to Oscar Lewis's account, Collis Huntington would later say that Stanford's total contribution to the Transcontinental Railroad consisted of turning over the first shovelful of earth and driving in the last spike, which, incidentally, he missed on the first swing.) Having just been released on payment of a $253,000 ransom, against an initial demand of $2.5 million, Thomas Durant was there for the Union Pacific side. (The best guess—and one certainly consistent with his character—is that Durant engineered his own abduction in order to secure the money necessary to pay off a contractor, who in turn made sure to feather Durant's own nest.) Durant missed on his first swing, too, much to the amusement of the Chinese and Irish laborers who had brought the track to this final union. Other dignitaries on both sides followed with their swings, often askew, and then the chief engineers finished the job, the continent was spanned with iron, and the officials could repair to Durant's gleaming Pullman car to recover before a luncheon aboard Stanford's car. As they did so, two locomotives, one representing each of the railroad companies, moved cautiously forward and touched cowcatchers to commemorate the moment. ("What was it the engines said," Bret Harte wondered in his *Overland Monthly*, "Pilots touching— head to head.")

It was aboard Thomas Durant's car that the Union Pacific's head engineer, Grenville Dodge, composed his moving telegraphic tribute to Abraham Lincoln under whose administration the railroad had begun "in the middle of a great rebellion" and to Ulysses Grant, Dodge's friend and fellow general from the war years, who had "conquered the peace." Dodge had been Theodore Judah's counterpart: Just as Judah had discovered the Donner Pass route through the Sierra Nevadas, the rugged, self-sufficient Dodge had found the route that carried the Union Pacific through the Rocky Mountains. The experience served him well, and not just for plotting track: A few years later, he was able to use his intimate knowledge of the newly opened American west to elude a process server who had chased him from Texas to St. Louis. Dodge, for whom Fort Dodge in Iowa is named, lived out his later years in a Victorian mansion in another Iowa city, Council Bluffs. He was said to be the richest man in the state, but like everyone associated with the Transcontinental Railroad, his reputation would forever be tainted by the Crédit Mobilier scandal. What it was possible to turn away from while the great project was underway became harder to ignore once the dust had settled.

Congress had been in the thick of the scandal, too: Crédit Mobilier stock had papered the place. To purge themselves, lawmakers scheduled a series of hearings meant, in theory, to bring the culpable among their own numbers to justice. Certain of how the hearings would turn out in practice, the *New York Sun* ran its account of the proceedings under the sardonic banner: "Trial of the Innocents." It wasn't quite that. Schuyler Colfax, who had been Speaker of the House while the railroad was being built and who had gone on to become Grant's vice president, fared poorly in the testimony, and two congressmen were censured, including Oakes Ames, who had been at the forefront of offering his colleagues steeply discounted shares in Crédit Mobilier.

Doc Durant, who had been in on the creation of Crédit Mobilier of America, escaped the legal consequences, but history caught up with him all the same. Wiped out by the succession of bank failures that launched the Panic of 1873, Durant tried to bounce back with an ultimately unsuccessful scheme to develop the iron and timber resources of the Adirondacks. He died there, half forgotten and far from rich, in 1885, 16 years after he had had the honor of driving in the final spike at Promontory Point.

⤳

Great acts are the fruit of great vision, not necessarily of great or moral people, but whatever America got cheated out of by the men who built the Transcontinental Railroad, she got back a thousand times over. Transportation was, of course, changed forever. The day the final spike was driven into the railroad in Promontory Summit, Wells Fargo, taking advantage of the almost completed track, had promised in a *New York Times* ad: "Seven days travel from the Missouri River to the Pacific Ocean," with only a single day's stagecoach riding. Soon, though, you could go all the way from New York to the West Coast in a week. On the iron horse instead of behind the real one multitudes could ride and bring their worldly possessions with them. And did they ever.

In the 18 years between the passage of the Railroad Act of 1862 and the U.S. Census of 1880, California's population grew 128 percent, to 865,000. Nebraska's population grew more than threefold between 1860 and 1870; Nevada's grew sixfold during the same time. Colorado had a bare 40,000 residents in 1870; by 1880 it had nearly 200,000. And Brigham Young had been right, too: Deseret, his promised land in the desert that became Utah, nearly doubled in population in the 11 years after the two railroads were finally joined there.

It wasn't just population that grew though. Rail begat rail, as the spider web of tracks that had characterized the eastern half of the nation before the Civil War came to characterize the nation as a whole. In 1869, a little more than four thousand miles of track were laid down across the country; three years later, by 1872, track was being laid down at the rate of nearly seventy five hundred miles a year. In all, railroads operated some fifty-three thousand miles of track in 1870; a decade later, they were running on more than ninety-three thousand miles of track, triple the figure only two decades earlier. The people tilled the new land and put up fences and mined the rich mountain mineral deposits, and the trains carried their grains and livestock and ore back East, where exports could be shipped overseas to the Old World that had lent much of the money to build the Transcontinental Railroad.

And it wasn't just trains and rail and commerce that expanded. It was attitude also. America had always been a place that promised wide open spaces. Now the wide open spaces were closer and easier to get to than they had ever been. In Collis Huntington, Mark Hopkins, Leland Stanford, Charles Crocker, and Thomas Durant—the men who had conquered the continent—there was also the promise that a man could go as far as his ambition would carry him, if only he was ruthless enough.

7

J. PIERPONT MORGAN

The American Colossus

B Y THE TIME ITS HUNDREDTH BIRTHDAY ROLLED around, America was ready to celebrate. The war had been over for more than a decade. The two coasts had been joined by rail seven years earlier, opening the vast western reaches of the nation for economic exploitation. Within six more years, another three railroads—the Northern Pacific, the Southern Pacific, and the Santa Fe—would join the Union Pacific and Central Pacific in offering service between the Midwest and the West Coast. If not empowered, African Americans were at least free. The great moral taint of slavery had begun to lift from the land. And after the twin shocks of the Panic of 1873 and the depression that followed, business was starting to boom again.

Government spending during the Civil War had brought rapid growth to the Northeast. Now, the good times were ready to spread out across the land. Oil speculators poured into western Pennsylvania and Ohio. Coal was leaving the ground as fast as men and machinery could extract it. Silver and gold mines opened in Colorado and throughout the Rocky Mountain states and territories. With markets growing for their products and with the means of transport readily at hand, manufacturers began to multiply their output. An 1869 government report declared:

> Within five years more cotton spindles had been put in motion, more iron furnaces erected, more iron smelted, more bars rolled, more steel made, more coal and copper mined, more lumber sawn and hewn, more houses and shops constructed, more manufactories of different kinds started, and more petroleum refined and exported, than during any equal period in the history of the country.

In fact, the party was just getting under way. As they had since the start of the Industrial Revolution, scientific progress and human prosperity seemed to be marching together. "Nine-tenths of the uncertainties [of making steel] were dispelled under the burning sun of chemical knowledge," Andrew Carnegie declared. Soon, railroads would be the prime supplier of the ore from which steel was made, the prime mover of the finished product, and the prime consumer of that product, too: a formula for unbridled prosperity for both parties.

On July 4, 1876, and during the weeks that followed, the nation celebrated its centennial by gathering in the city where its Founding Fathers had met to launch this bold experiment in democratic capitalism. And like the nation that had grown up in the 100 years since, the Centennial Exposition in Philadelphia was huge. Two hundred fifty-six acres of Fairmount Park were enclosed by fence for the event. Patrons—and ten million of them, a quarter of the nation's population, showed up—paid 50 cents each to enter through 13 gates, one for each original colony. Inside were 190 separate buildings, a full 50 acres under cover. The main building alone was three times the length of Grand Central Station and boasted 11.5 miles of aisles. Walking the whole exposition, from building to building and down all the aisles of each, meant wearing out 25 miles worth of shoe leather. For patrons who tired, a narrow-gauge railroad circumnavigated the grounds. France contributed 700 paintings to the art exhibition in Memorial Hall. Queen Victoria of England sent along a napkin she had woven to be shown in the Woman's Pavilion. At the center of Machinery Hall stood a twin, 2,500-horsepower Corliss engine, more than 40 feet tall, weighing over 600 tons, and capable of powering some 8,000 gadgets scattered around the hall.

In all, the Centennial Exposition painted a portrait of a nation about to step into its greatness. Across the Atlantic, though, a different picture prevailed. To continue growing, the U.S. economy needed capital investment, yet to most investors in Europe, where the great majority of wealth still resided, the New World of the mid-to-late 1800s seemed much closer to the Third World of today, filled with immense opportunity and with immense risk, each in equal and unsettling measure. Tainted by Crédit Mobilier and other scandals, American businessmen had about them the general odor of unreliability, well earned in many cases. America itself remained deeply in debt, still crippled by the cost of waging a war to preserve the union. With nothing approaching the Federal Reserve system of today, American banking was also inherently unstable, subject to a cyclical barrage of panics, bank runs, inflation, and depression.

Investment is never without peril, but unless investors have reason to trust the probity and wisdom of those they are entrusting their money to, they are not likely to crack their wallets very far. As Cosimo de' Medici had shown four centuries earlier, reputation counts, and in the late nineteenth century, no figure in American finance had a more towering reputation than J. Pierpont Morgan, known to friend and foe alike as "Jupiter"—ruler of the skies, the biggest of the big. Without ever holding a government title, J.P. Morgan would preside over a massive transfer of capital from Europe to the United States, and without ever manufacturing a thing, he would help create the modern industrial economy. In the twilight of his years, he would even rescue the New York Stock Exchange, virtually on his own.

~~

For all that has been written about him, John Pierpont Morgan continues to resist definition. He was a pillar of the Episcopal Church, and a generous supporter of good causes. In life, he had subsidized a new edition of the Book of Common Prayer and much more—he gave half a million dollars to the church in 1892 alone. He read the Bible by himself, and busied himself with church policy. At the end, he reaffirmed his piety (and his self-confidence) in a will that famously began: "I commit my soul into the hands of my savior in full confidence that having redeemed it and washed it in His most precious blood, He will present it faultless before my heavenly father. . . ." The Pope himself expressed great distress at Morgan's death in Rome, in March 1913, after he had fallen gravely ill in Cairo. And yet, even if he was a god of money, "Jupiter" Morgan was no saint.

His first wife had been Amelia Sturges, the daughter of a wealthy New York merchant and arts patron. They were both 20 when they fell in love in New York City in 1857. Four years later they were married in her parents' parlor; by then, though, Amelia was so ill that Morgan had to hold her up at the altar. In Paris, where her condition was finally determined to be tuberculosis, Morgan would carry her up and down seven flights of stairs a day so she could lead what passed for a normal life, all to no avail. Four months after the wedding, Alice Sturges—by all accounts a lively, intelligent woman—died. In some ways, says Morgan's biographer Jean Strouse, he would never get over the loss. Morgan was married again three years later, just after Lincoln's assassination, to Frances Louisa Tracy, but it was a union that never seemed to work. He liked crowds, the city, hard work, and the perks that go with life on the center stage. As his own wealth mounted, he became a serious patron of the arts. She wanted a quiet suburban life; art didn't interest her.

They were to remain married until her death, but by 1880 or so, Morgan was regularly putting an ocean between himself and Fanny, as Frances was known. He would spend the spring and summer in Europe, often with a mistress; when he returned, Fanny would depart for Europe with one of their daughters, a chauffeur, and a paid companion. More mistresses would follow, in New York and elsewhere, along with the occasional show girl—more than occasional, if the gossip is to be believed. Morgan spent $1 million to build the Lying Inn maternity hospital in New York City and gave $100,000 a year to it for the rest of his life. The logical explanation for this generosity is that the obstetrician who oversaw the facility was J.P. Morgan's best friend, but the wags and tattlers contended the hospital's principal job was to see to the pregnancies of Morgan's conquests.

Power, as has always been said, is a powerful aphrodisiac, and Morgan had power to burn, both in his vaults and in his person. The great photographer Edward Steichen said that looking into Morgan's eyes was like staring into the headlights of an oncoming locomotive. If you couldn't step off the tracks, Steichen said, it was terrifying. A woman who had known him told Jean Strouse that when Morgan "walked into a room, you felt something electric. He was like the king. He was 'it.'"

Morgan had a reputation, too, as an imperious man, and he had the trappings to prove it. There was the art collection worth in the tens of millions of dollars; the town house at Madison Avenue and 36th Street in Manhattan that he had bought in 1880; the library next door that he had Charles McKim design in the early 1900s to house his great book collection; Cragston, the country house up the Hudson River;

and perhaps most splendid of all the yachts that carried him between town and country, and from continent to continent. They were all called *Corsair,* and each was bigger than the last. He bought the first *Corsair,* a 183-foot beauty, in 1882. When Jay Gould and James Gordon Bennett showed up with longer yachts, Morgan sold the first *Corsair* and had a second one built, at 241 feet, and when that was requisitioned for the Spanish-American War, he had a third made, at somewhere over 280 feet—a yacht nearly as long as a football field.

Yet for all the high living and the blue blood—and he had plenty of that, too—Morgan was in many ways more a meritocrat than an aristocrat. He was constantly searching for competent, interesting, original people, and when he found them, he would provide them the resources to do what they were best at, whatever their background. Capable of playing the bully, he also understood quality and gave its lead.

His librarian Belle Greene, who traveled far and wide over Europe searching out new purchases and who seems to have had his absolute trust, had been born Belle Greener. Her father, Jean Strouse discovered in researching *Morgan: American Financier,* had been the first black man to graduate from Harvard University. Greene appears to have passed her whole life as white, but Strouse suspects that had Morgan learned of her racial background, he wouldn't have minded: Once he found talent, he stuck by it. It's no accident either that when Thomas Edison first began furnishing electricity to customers from his Pearl Street generating station in lower Manhattan, the very first place to be electrified—at exactly 3 P.M. on September 4, 1882—was the Wall Street office of J. Pierpont Morgan. Half James Watt and half Matthew Boulton, Edison had an entrepreneurial flair to go along with his inventive genius, and Morgan knew a good idea when he saw one.

Morgan was the great financier of his time, one of America's most public men. Presidents consulted him. On his frequent European trips, he consorted with lords and ladies. At home, he could barely walk across the street from his office at 23 Wall Street without causing at least a ripple of speculation. He was also painfully shy; thoroughly inarticulate with his business partners; private, almost secretive in his deliberations; and extremely volatile when crossed.

"He was famous for his few words, Yes or No," the novelist John Dos Passos wrote in his portrait of Morgan in *Nineteen-Nineteen*, "and for his way of suddenly blowing up in a visitor's face and for that special gesture of the arm that meant, *What do I get out of it?*"

Jupiter had been sickly as a child, suffering from seizures, sore throats, and headaches. In his teen years, he was plagued by an aggressive acne that probably presaged the rhinophyma that would so disfigure his nose in later years. At fifteen, he was sent off to the Azores by himself to recover from rheumatic fever, and the loneliness seems to have initiated a depression that would recur throughout his life. As an adult, Morgan would make decisions that would move markets and change the face of industry, but the mechanics of the decisions remained a mystery even to his intimates. One of his partners said, "He's an impossible man to have any talk with. The nearest approach he makes is an occasional grunt." A close friend described him as "very intuitive and instinctive. He couldn't sit down and rationally analyze a problem. Or if he could, he couldn't tell you about it." When the going got really tough, Morgan would retreat by himself to his inner office with two packs of cards to play a double-deck solitaire game called Mrs. Milliken, and somehow in the repetition of laying the cards out and moving them around, answers would suggest themselves to him, often great and epic answers.

He helped save the United States and perhaps the global economy three times—the panics of 1873 and 1893 and the Wall Street crisis of 1907—and all three bailouts further enhanced his stature and reputation and made the world more willing to trust its money with J. P. Morgan. "War and panics on the stock exchange, bankruptcies, warloans good growing weather for the House of Morgan," Dos Passos wrote, but it was never as simple as that.

⁓

He didn't just stumble into banking. His father, Junius Spencer Morgan, was a highly successful merchant, with offices in Hartford, Connecticut—where Pierpont was born in 1837—and later in Boston. Junius Morgan, though, had larger ambitions. He wanted to create in America what the Rothschilds and Baring brothers had in Europe: not just powerful bankers, but a dynasty with tentacles reaching through the entire global banking business and into every corner of American industry. It was to that end that Junius Morgan set himself up in London in 1854: He would be the starting end of the conduit that would facilitate the transfer of European wealth to the New World. The Rothschilds had missed the historic moment; they had one agent in America to handle their business there. The Barings had also failed to move aggressively into the American market: The potential high rewards of investing there came so often with unacceptably high risks. Junius Morgan wouldn't miss the moment, and in his son, John Pierpont, he would offer European investors all the assurance they needed that the money they were sending across the ocean would be in safe and responsible hands when it arrived. To make that assurance he had first to train his son in all the right attitudes.

The first lesson was: No speculative investments. And Junius Morgan, who seems to have spared his son no criticism, taught it with a vengeance. "How could you be so reckless and crazy?" he's said to have once screamed at Pierpont when he ventured into five shares of the Pacific Mall and Steamship Company. The lesson was driven home when the son held on to the shares against his father's will and eventually had to sell them for a loss.

The second lesson flowed from the first: A man who was prone to speculation could not be trusted with the capital of others because, finally, trust was built on character and reputation. In the last year of life, testifying before a House of Representatives Committee convened to investigate the inordinate control Morgan exercised over the nation's economic life, Jupiter condensed this lesson for Congress: Credit, he told committee members, is not based primarily upon money or property "The first thing is character [and that] money cannot buy.... A man I do not trust could not get money from me on all the bones of Christendom."

And from those two lessons, everything else flowed as well: To be trustworthy, you had to be prudent. To be prudent meant exercising control. And to exercise control effectively, you had to concentrate capital. Put all three together, and you have the process that came to be known as Morganization.

The railroads were the first to be Morganized. They were entering the period of their greatest growth as J.P. Morgan turned 30, in 1867, and thus the time of their greatest need for investment capital. The railroads were also the linchpin that would finally solidify the scatter-shot American economy. Without them, there was no national market nor any effective way to connect raw materials, manufacturers, and consumers in a timely or economic fashion. And the railroads also desperately needed what the merchant bank overseen by Junius Morgan and his son was prepared to offer in such abundance: character, reputation, and probity. Crédit Mobilier had been only the most spectacular of a series of railroad frauds dating back into the 1830s.

To raise the money to finance the building of the rail-roads, the Morgan Bank sold bonds, primarily to European investors and mostly through its London offices. To assure that the holders of those bonds wouldn't be burned, the Morgan Bank in America would carefully monitor the progress of the railroads in whose names the bonds had been issued. If one went bankrupt, Jupiter himself would move in—in the exercise of his fiduciary responsibilities—fire the incompetent brass, hire new managers, reorganize the company, restructure its finances, and finally appoint a new board of directors, always including those who understood his will and often including himself as the prime translator of his own desires.

In time, the weak sisters among the railroads—those who couldn't attract new capital, often because they couldn't win the trust of J.P. Morgan—were driven out of business. As that happened, an industry that had been characterized more than anything else by savage, often self-destructive competition began to concentrate itself into fewer and fewer entities, many of them reorganized by Morgan himself: the Baltimore & Ohio Railroad, for example, and the Northern Pacific. Where side wars threatened to upset the harmony of the whole that he was creating, Morgan personally intervened to restore peace—most notably in the running skirmishes between Pennsylvania railroads and coal producers in that coal-rich state. Thus, the influence of the Morgan Bank spread throughout the railroad industry: By the start of the new century, Morgan had some five thousand miles of rail under his financial control. Thus, too, the investors who had trusted in the Morgan Bank were repaid for their faith: Concentrated control meant that capital could be put to work reproducing itself, rather than endlessly fending off competition. And thus the power of the bank (and of Morgan) grew nearly exponentially.

What worked for rails worked for the fledgling electric industry, too, and for farm equipment, steel, and communications: Almost a century after J.P. Morgan's death, his imprint is still all over the New York Stock Exchange Big Board. Ten years after Thomas Alva Edison had first illuminated Morgan's Wall Street office, Morgan put together the financing that created General Electric, the only component of the original Dow Jones Industrial Average, first published in 1896, still a part of the average a hundred years later. International Harvester followed, as did AT&T, both Morgan-backed creations meant to concentrate control and eliminate cutthroat competition. In 1901, Morgan created the syndicate that paid Andrew Carnegie $480 million for his steel company—Carnegie himself got $240 million of the deal. Carnegie Steel, in turn, became the centerpiece of perhaps the greatest of Morgan's industrial creations: U.S. Steel, the first billion-dollar corporation and an industry giant for decades to come.

While the deals multiplied, the name on the door simplified. He had started his career in 1857 with Duncan, Sherman, and Company in New York City; moved on to George Peabody & Co. and from there to head the firm named for his father: J.S. Morgan. In 1864, J.S. Morgan had folded into Dabney, Morgan, & Co. and later Drexel, Morgan, & Co. In 1895, the firm became simply J.P. Morgan and Co.—a colossus named for a colossus.

As great as J.P. Morgan's role was in shaping the modern industrial economy, his greater legacy may have been in quelling the financial panics that periodically swept the nation. Morgan had been born during the second administration of Andrew Jackson, just as Old Hickory was succeeding in dismantling the Second Bank of the United States. Morgan would die less than eight months before the Federal Reserve System was created—created in large part out of public shock at the range of Morgan's power over America's economic life. In between, for almost the exact span of Morgan's life, there was no central bank other than J.P. Morgan.

John Kenneth Galbraith has noted that panics settled upon the American economy about every twenty years throughout the nineteenth century, just about the length of time it took for the public to forget about the last one. The Panic of 1873 had been ignited by the failure of a leading Philadelphia bank, Jay Cooke and Company, but Cooke himself had fallen victim to an overheated economy and deteriorating conditions in Europe, which still exercised a powerful influence over America's financial life. Twenty years later, in 1893, panic was ready to strike again, just as Grover Cleveland was beginning his second term. This time the contributing factors were a lengthy depression, a sharp decline in foreign trade brought on by the enactment of the McKinley tariff, and a high general burden of private debt, but the trigger was a number anyone could follow: the level of gold reserves in the federal treasury. The assumption was that $100 million was the baseline number: the amount necessary to assure that government obligations would be redeemed in gold. When the reserves fell below that line for the first time on April 21, 1893, a panic began that would rage on for more than two years, toppling banks and businesses and driving the nation as a whole into a deep depression.

Morgan had played the pivotal role in turning around the 1873 panic, arranging for a bond issue that allowed the federal government to meet its financial obligations. Now, two decades later, Grover Cleveland turned to him as perhaps the only person in America capable of restoring confidence in the public purse. John Dos Passos described the moment:

In the panic of '93 at no inconsiderable profit to himself Morgan saved the U.S. Treasury. Gold was draining out, the country was ruined, the farmers were howling for a silver standard, Grover

Cleveland and his cabinet were walking up and down in the blue room at the White House without being able to come to a decision, in Congress they were making speeches while the gold reserves melted in the Subtreasuries; poor people were starving; Coxey's army was marching to Washington; for a long time Grover Cleveland couldn't bring himself to call in the representative of the Wall Street moneymasters; Morgan sat in his suite at the Arlington smoking cigars and quietly playing solitaire until at the last the president sent for him; he had a plan all ready for stopping the gold hemorrhage.

After that what Morgan said went.

Morgan's plan was both the height of simplicity and a measure of how thoroughly he and the institution he had created stood at the crossroads of the nation's economic life. As America's de facto lender of last resort, the Morgan Bank would lend the U.S. Treasury $62 million in gold in 1895. Added to the $38 million in gold reserves left in the Treasury, the nation would again have a reserve of $100 million. With that, public confidence started to build and the panic ended. The lessons, though, were slow as always to sink in. In a little more than a decade, the nation would be teetering on the brink of ruin yet again.

⤚⤙

Morgan was 70 years old in October 1907, lost in the minutiae of his beloved Episcopalian church at a denominational convention near Richmond, Virginia, when a series of telegrams arrived from his office. Under the pressure of tumbling stock prices, several prominent brokerage houses had been forced to close their doors. Danger of the worst sort lay ahead for Wall Street and the stock exchange unless the tide could be reversed. In Congress, conservative lawmakers were lambasting Teddy Roosevelt for the problems: His trust-busting and excessive regulation, they claimed, were leading big business to ruin. At the Morgan Bank, which had helped create many of the businesses under assault by Roosevelt, a more profound and immediate truth prevailed: If prominent brokerage houses had already gone under in the crisis, lesser ones were sure to follow, in abundance. Once that happened, the deluge would be on. The stock market would collapse, and the national economy with it.

By today's terms, the situation was almost certainly containable. The Federal Reserve Board, the secretary of the treasury, and the president all have macro- and micro-economic tools at their immediate disposal that a turn-of-the-century economist or political leader could barely imagine; and the stock exchanges have brakes of their own to build breathing room into a selling panic. In 1907, though, just as in 1893 to 1895, there seemed to be only one solution, and it was entirely extra-governmental. For what was to be a final time, Jupiter—J.P. Morgan—would come to the rescue.

Morgan waited until the church convention ended that weekend, then rushed back to New York City by private railroad car, drawn by a night train. Anything more rash, he had been told, was likely to spook an already scared market. He spent Sunday in his library, surrounded by business partners and lieutenants. By Monday, the New York financial district was in turmoil. Thousands thronged the streets, trying to get their money out of the banks. Managers had instructed tellers to count money in slow motion, but the tedious delay only accentuated the crisis. As banks around the nation withdrew their reserves from New York, the panic broadened and the danger spread. Morgan had been back in town less than a week when New York officials came to him with news that the city couldn't meet its own payroll obligations and would have to declare bankruptcy the next Monday. To fend off that likelihood, he came up with $100 million worth of commercial bank loans, but that didn't help Wall Street.

For nearly three weeks Morgan's team had been assessing financial institutions, deciding which should be left to fail and which were strong and well-managed enough to merit help. For the latter group, he and other financiers raised hundreds of millions of dollars in support, including loans from the same U.S. Treasury that Morgan had helped to rescue a dozen years earlier. As the panic wore on, Morgan himself began to wear down. He'd scarcely eaten for three days and was suffering from a terrible cold when the head of the Stock Exchange crossed the street to Morgan's office to tell him that the exchange would have to close. Morgan shook his head in response: Shutting down the stock exchange, he said, would lead to a widespread depression. Instead, he gathered the leading bankers in New York together in his library—the men who controlled the money that Wall Street lived off of—and presented them with a stark proposition: "We need $20 million in the next ten minutes," Morgan said, "or the stock exchange will have to close early." For added emphasis, Morgan is said to have locked the library doors, vowing no man would leave until all the money was pledged. From someone else it might have been a bluff, but as had been the case with J.P. Morgan for more than forty years, his reputation preceded him, and his character as well. The bank presidents capitulated, and the Panic of 1907 turned the corner and began to end.

As news of the rescue circulated through the Stock Exchange, Morgan could hear a roar across the street. The mighty and feared Jupiter was being given an ovation by the jubilant floor traders.

For J.P. Morgan & Company there would be other chances to ride to the aid of the nation, if not to save it. Morgan's son, J.P. Jr., would oversee a syndicate that raised another $100 million to preserve New York City's credit in 1913. During World War I the Allies borrowed nearly $1.9 billion through the company; afterwards Morgan & Company floated loans of nearly $1.7 billion for European reconstruction. For Jupiter himself, though, the Panic of 1907 was the last hurrah.

"For about a minute he was regarded as a national hero," his biographer Jean Strouse told an interviewer. "Crowds cheered when he walked down Wall Street, and world political leaders and bankers sent telegrams expressing their awe that one man had been able to do that. But the next minute a democratic nation was really quite horrified at the idea that one man had this much power."

Rather than trust its fate again to a single citizen, the United States established the Federal Reserve system in 1913, returning to a form of the central bank it had abandoned almost eighty years earlier. From now on, the nation would be its own lender of last resort, and the governors of the system would be appointed by the President and answerable to Congress. A century that had begun with John Pierpont Morgan as the absolute czar of American finance would end with Alan Greenspan filling that role—the difference great not only in degree but in kind. Even if he had a desire to, the enigmatic Greenspan could never move markets the way Morgan could by a simple grunt or lifting of his arm.

Congress caught the spirit of a people who had decided Jupiter's time had passed. What had seemed a grand benevolence suddenly had become a stranglehold on credit and capital, and Americans have never trusted concentrated wealth. In 1911, Louisiana Representative Arsane Pujo opened congressional hearings on money trusts and their affect on the common weal. In December 1912, already past his 75th birthday, J.P. Morgan appeared before the panel. Not surprisingly, he didn't yield an inch. Less than four months later, he was dead.

In its editorial extolling the fallen financier, the *New York Times* of April 1, 1913, caught the spirit of both the man and the history he had lived through and helped create.

We may look upon Mr. Morgan's like again—there were great men before and after Agamennon, but we shall not look upon another career like his. The time for that has gone by. Conditions have changed, and Mr. Morgan, the mighty and dominant figure of finance, did more than any other man to change them. Forty years ago, when he was coming to prominence here and abroad, Wall Street was in the stage of youth and promise. There was no money power then; by far the greater part of the Nation's present wealth has been created since that day.

Mr. Morgan was born for leadership, for constructive work. With his unmatched abilities, with his character and the confidence he inspired, and with his power to organize and command, it was inevitable that he should be the leader, the builder-up in the domain on American finance. The growth in his time was prodigious, and now Wall Street is beyond the need or the possibility of one-man leadership. There will be co-ordination of effort, the union of resources, but Mr. Morgan will have no successor; there will be no one man to whom all will look for direction.

The *Times* estimated J.P. Morgan's fortune at "near $100,000,000," including art and other collectibles with a worth of anywhere from $30 million to $60 million. Later estimates downplayed the figure to about $80 million. Either way, it was a tremendous fortune perhaps equaling $1.5 billion to $3 billion in current dollars. One man, though, wasn't impressed. Having read the *Times* account of Morgan's assets, he is said to have shook his head and commented, "And to think, he wasn't even a rich man." The story is almost certainly apocryphal—it's too good to be true—but the man the quote is attributed to is anything but made up: John Davison Rockefeller.

8

JOHN D. ROCKEFELLER

Organizing the Octopus

N 1861, AT THE START OF THE CIVIL WAR, NO American company had achieved a market capitalization as high as $10 million. By the start of the twentieth century, 300 companies had. The largest of them, U.S. Steel, had a market cap of $1.4 billion, this at a time when the annual gross national product barely topped $20 billion. Under the stern tutelage of J.P. Morgan, American business was consolidating. A nation of shop owners, craftsmen, and small manufacturers was becoming a nation of shop clerks, factory workers, and sprawling corporations. In metals, transportation, utilities, and other sectors, the cutthroat competition that traditionally characterizes industries in their formative years—much like the technology industry today—was giving way to cutthroat trusts.

The great trusts of the late 1800s were necessary legal creations. Under the laws of the day, corporations could not own stock in businesses located outside their state of incorporation. To allow a company to operate nationally, individual shareholders in aligned corporations would surrender their stock to a group of trustees and receive trust certificates in return. By the turn of the century, though, almost no one thought of trusts in their fine legal sense. "Trusts" had come to be synonymous with "monopolies": They combined separate—but, in fact, inseparable—entities under a single leadership not to facilitate interstate business or achieve economies of scale but to eliminate and, if necessary, ruthlessly stamp out competition.

This consolidation of control inevitably meant a consolidation of wealth. The more broadly a corporation spread itself over all aspects of its business, the more it could control prices paid to suppliers, prices charged to customers, and labor and production costs. Inevitably, too, the consolidated wealth flowed most freely and generously to the top of the trusts, where the greatest control was exercised. America had produced plenty of fortunes in her first hundred years—the land was too plentiful to do otherwise—but with the creation of trusts, the nation launched a new breed of the super-rich. Collectively, they came to be known by a useful phrase first introduced into the language in 1872: robber barons.

The history of the twentieth century tends to be written in terms of political leaders: Wilson, Churchill, Stalin, Hitler, Franklin Roosevelt, John Kennedy, Mao Zedong—they bestrode their times like colossi. The nineteenth century was different, especially the closing decades. After the assassination of Lincoln and the presidential follies of his successors Andrew Johnson and the war hero Ulysses Grant, politicians disappear from American history. Rutherford B. Hayes, James Garfield, Chester Alan Arthur, the two separate Grover Cleveland administrations, Benjamin Harrison, William McKinley—who even remembers them anymore, except as footnotes in the long, sad history of presidential assassinations? In an era of Big Business, not Big Politics, it was businessmen who drove their times, and the robber barons more so than any of them. Astor, Carnegie, Cooke, Gould, Harrison, Hill, Huntington, Morgan, Stanford, Vanderbilt—those are the names that define the history of the latter part of the nineteenth century. To them, politicians were at best a necessary evil, people to be paid off to be kept out of the way.

Two factors, though, were working to change that equation as the twentieth century dawned. One was a crusading journalist named Ida Tarbell, who starting in 1902 began to publish a series of highly popular articles in *McClure's Magazine* under the deceptively bland title "A History of Standard Oil." The articles, which continued for nearly three years, laid out in astoundingly accurate, poignant, and sometimes almost lurid detail the inner workings of one of the most powerful and ruthlessly assembled of all the trusts. At the same time, Teddy Roosevelt, nearing the end of his first elected term as president, was looking for an unrepentant trust to bust. Tarbell handed him Standard Oil for the purpose. The government had been pursuing the oil giant in the courts ever since the Sherman Antitrust Act was passed in 1890; under Roosevelt, though, the court case would become part and parcel of his political ambition, the makings of a crusade. For good measure Tarbell threw into the mix the man her articles had helped turn into the most reviled man in America, and one of the most loathed people in the world: Standard Oil's own robber baron, John Davison Rockefeller. For Rockefeller, who refused to dignify the *McClure's* series with a rebuttal, Teddy Roosevelt's efforts to ratchet up antitrust action must have added insult to injury: He had contributed $250,000—equivalent to more than $1 million today—to the McKinley-Roosevelt campaign in 1896, precisely so this wouldn't occur.

Like Morgan, Rockefeller was a man of relentless contradictions, almost all of them carried to an absolute extreme. The philosopher William James, brother of Henry and one of the great intellects of his age, said that John D. Rockefeller was the most strongly bad and strongly good human being he had ever met, and also one of the most suggestive and formidable personalities: "A man 10 stories deep," he wrote

149

to Henry, "and to me quite unfathomable...superficially suggestive of naught but goodness and conscientiousness, yet accused of being the greatest villain in business whom our country has produced."

From his mother, Eliza, Rockefeller had inherited a fierce piety; a moral strictness that stressed thrift, industriousness, and discipline; and a powerful social conscience. Morgan and Rockefeller were both of fighting age when the Civil War broke out, and each would buy his way out of service in the Civil War for $300—in the North, the practice was common among those who had the wherewithal. But unlike Morgan and his father, for whom the war was largely seen as a business inconvenience, Rockefeller was neither unconcerned with nor immune to the most volatile issues of the time. Not only was he an abolitionist himself; he married into a family of ardent abolitionists—people who had been conductors on the Underground Railroad and who had sheltered Sojourner Truth in their house.

Indeed, in Laura "Cetti" Spelman, his wife of 50 years, Rockefeller seems to have found his mother incarnate. Like Eliza, she was a teetotaler and a model of piety, habits that great wealth seemed to ingrain still more deeply. Eventually, the Rockefellers would have four estates to choose from, some with beautiful bridle paths and all with a nine-hole golf course so John D. could indulge in his favorite pastime. Inside, though, there was almost nothing frivolous. J.P. Morgan adorned his mansions with great art, jeweled snuff boxes, and actresses whom he liked to have call him "Commodore." The Rockefellers seem to have furnished theirs with the kind of dourness that is so often a handmaiden to an overpowering religiosity. Nothing went to waste, not even affection. John D. Jr., their only son, once commented that he had worn only female clothing until he was eight years old—hand-me-downs from his older sisters. As the public image of her husband worsened, Cetti appears to have been driven ever more into the church for refuge, but she had a conscience of her own to exercise, and the money to do it with. Begun as a school for the education of freed Negro women, Spelman College in Atlanta bears the maiden name of its greatest benefactor.

From his father, Rockefeller inherited opposite talents, including a capacity for low cunning and schemery. William "Devil Bill" Rockefeller was a snake-oil salesman and a bigamist. He traveled the Northeast selling worthless curing potions, assuming a series of identities from "botanic physician," to "celebrated cancer specialist," to that of an impoverished deaf mute. Finally, about 1855, Devil Bill abandoned the Rockefeller family for good, marrying a much younger woman who knew him only as Dr. William Livingston. In the almost fifty years of his second marriage, Rockefeller's biographer Ron Chernow learned, William Rockefeller would periodically drop out of the blue into his son's life, but his wife, Margaret Allen Livingston, would learn only in the final years of her life that her husband was the father of the world's richest man.

John D. also seems to have added a certain ruthlessness and unsentimentality to the qualities inherited from his father. He once memorably warned his wife that "A man who succeeds in life must sometimes go against the current," and he seems to have set out to prove that axiom every day in his business dealings. "You may not be afraid to have your hand cut off," he warned one competitor, "but your body will suffer." When threats didn't work, he rigged deals. When that didn't work, he bought people, or at least their votes, and the support of newspapers, too. One Ohio senator was paid $44,000 in "lobbying fees" to discredit a state attorney general who was harassing Standard Oil; Rockefeller's records suggest it was almost common practice. And because he was both his mother's and his father's child, he spent inordinate hours both plotting out his actions and justifying them in his own private view of theology.

J.P. Morgan had acted by instinct; Rockefeller acted almost by its opposite. He was a man of relentless repetition: As he got older, Rockefeller played golf at the same time every morning, chewed each bite ten times before swallowing as part of a pre-New Age health ritual, and swirled liquids in his mouth ten times before swallowing for the same reason. He was also a man of enormous will power, and he rarely failed to get what he wanted. One of his goals had been to reach his 100th birthday, and he almost made it, dying in 1937, at age 98. Another of his goals had been to dominate oil from the wellhead to the marketplace. That he did with astounding success and in the process grew wealthier than any businessman had ever been. Yet in a time that celebrated greed, Rockefeller seemed to have gone one step too far.

Burdened with a pinch-penny's face and legendary for the single thin dimes he would hand out to children as an old man, John D. Rockefeller also practically wrote the book on how to put a great fortune to public use. He had tithed even as a teenager, giving to his Baptist church. By the time he was rich beyond reckoning, he was giving money away almost as fast as he made it. The best estimates are that in his lifetime Rockefeller and the foundation named after him donated more than $530 million to charitable causes—a fortune then, a far greater fortune in today's dollars. The University of Chicago alone got $35 million. Through his Rockefeller Sanitary Commission, he helped eradicate hookworm disease in the South, what one historian called "the germ of laziness," in part through the simple expedient of handing out shoes by the tens of thousands. Through the Rockefeller Institute for Medical Research, now Rockefeller University, the first institute in the world devoted solely to medical research, he helped confront far more complex diseases head on.

This son of a bigamist and snake-oil merchant also founded one of America's most distinguished and generous families. John D. Jr. would devote his life to philanthropic and civic causes, giving away another $400 million, including buying up the lands that were to become Grand Teton and Acadia national parks and donating them to the federal government that had tried so hard to destroy his father. "I believe that every right implies a responsibility; every opportunity, an obligation; every possession, a duty," John D. Jr. told a gathering of the United Service Organization on the eve of World War II. Happiness seems to have eluded him, but the call to service was almost a vocation for his own children. Nelson, who was born on the same day as his famous grandfather, would become governor of New York, a frequent candidate for the Republican presidential nomination, and vice president of the United States, nominated by Gerald Ford to succeed himself after the resignation of Richard Nixon. Winthrop was governor of Arkansas and a distinguished stockman, as well as board chairman of Colonial Williamsburg, which his father had been instrumental in founding. Laurance, a noted conservationist, donated the lands that led to the creation of the Virgin Islands National Park. John D. III headed up the Rockefeller Foundation, amassed one of the world's great collections of Oriental art, and funded New York City's Lincoln Center for the Performing Arts; and David was chairman of Chase Manhattan Bank and the Council on Foreign Relations as well as a major benefactor of the Museum of Modern Art, another Rockefeller family project. At this writing, the original John D.'s great-grandson and namesake, John D. IV, is serving his third term as a Democratic senator from West Virginia.

Photos of John D. Rockefeller always seemed to make him seem so short—that thin face, under that copious top hat—but in fact he was tall for his time, all of six feet. Maybe that's one reason it was so easy to underestimate him.

◦≋◦

J.P. Morgan had been born into a rich business that just got bigger and richer under his watch. John D. Rockefeller, by contrast, lived the economic saga of his times. He'd begun his work life in 1855, at age 16, as a bookkeeper with a Cleveland merchant house. In 1858, he quit to start a partnership called Clark & Rockefeller, a small grocery firm in an era characterized by such low-scale businesses. Five years later, still a grocer, Rockefeller made a $4,000 dollar investment in a fledgling Cleveland oil refinery. That was in 1863, when the petroleum business was the industrial equivalent of the wild, wild West.

The first oil field in the world had been discovered just seven years earlier, in 1856 by Col. Edwin Drake in Titusville, Pennsylvania, and it was still the only one. The demobilization of troops following the Civil War would give the business the one thing it was missing up to then: a new army of toughened young men out to make their fortunes. By 1870, when Rockefeller founded the Standard Oil Company in Cleveland, Titusville and the surrounding cities—places with names like Oil City—literally stank with crude and crawled with the men who brought it in, or failed to. Hundreds of derricks had been sunk, nearly all of them the work of individual companies. Because crude oil is virtually useless unless its refined, hundreds of refineries also sprang up at the other end of the industrial pipeline. In Cleveland alone, Rockefeller's Standard Oil was one of 26 refineries fighting for survival in a highly uncertain and hugely volatile single-source market: During the decade of the 1860s, the price of crude went as high at $13 a barrel and as low as 10 cents.

Rockefeller, in short, wasn't the first to realize the economic potential of the new industry. America was booming in population and economic vitality. Refined into kerosene, oil could help heat homes and light the streets of fast-growing cities. It could also power machinery, including the machinery that was the infrastructure of the newly connected nation. Steam-driven locomotives served by coal tenders were a constant fire threat in the dry and delicate grasslands of the American prairie; steam locomotives powered by oil tenders were not.

Rockefeller probably also wasn't the first to realize that in a business sense, oil wasn't even the key part of the oil-refining industry. All oil from the same oil field—and there was only one—was essentially the same in physical properties. It essentially cost the same within any given moment in the widely fluctuating market. And all refining processes were largely the same, too. Impurities were being removed to make the crude usable; there was no value-added component to separate finished products in the marketplace. What created the critical cost difference in such a margin-driven industry was transportation. The cheaper a refiner could get the oil from the field to his refinery and from his refinery to the market and consumer, the more margin he had to play with. Conversely, the more expensive he could make transportation for his competitors, the less they had to play with.

For the pious and analytical side of John D. Rockefeller, such a realization practically had the force of scripture: Solve the transportation riddle in your favor, and you could bring order to one of America's most chaotic free markets. Otherwise, oil would always be an unacceptably volatile industry. "The oil business was in confusion and daily growing worse," he would later explain. "Someone had to take a stand." For Rockefeller's cunning and scheming side, the realization also seems to have had an irresistible draw: Solve the transportation riddle, and you could crush your competition and dictate the terms of their surrender. Rockefeller would do both.

Through a conspiracy known as the South Improvement Company, Rockefeller made a pact with three railroad companies: They would get the lion's share of all oil traffic. In exchange, Standard Oil would be granted preferential rail rates at the same time that its competitors in the refinery business were being saddled with punitive rates. The pact was a secret one, but the secret didn't keep for long. As word leaked out in western Pennsylvania, torch-wielding mobs of refiners moved from Titusville to Franklin, Oil City, and other oil-field towns, rioting, tearing railroad tracks apart, and raiding Standard Oil cars. Rockefeller had been barely known beyond his own business circle: The South Improvement Company deal would cause his name to appear in newsprint for the first time. Now, he was the "Mephistopheles of Cleveland"—and he was far from through.

Barely two months after it was formed, the courts ruled Rockefeller's secret pact illegal. Before that happened, though, Rockefeller had already moved in for the kill. In less than 6 weeks, Standard Oil swallowed up 22 of its 26 Cleveland competitors, all at rock-bottom prices. Among the oil men ruined in what came to be known as "the Cleveland Massacre" was the father of Ida Tarbell, the journalist whose *McClure* articles would so inspire Teddy Roosevelt to go after the man responsible.

As Standard Oil gained momentum, the Cleveland acquisitions were followed in quick order by others. Rockefeller would pick up 53 refineries in all and close down 32 of them, retaining only the most efficient. Thus the momentum grew even greater—thanks to its new economies of scale, Standard Oil could cut the cost of refining oil by two-thirds, from 1.5 cents a gallon to .5 cents a gallon—and as momentum grew, market share soared.

JOHN D. ROCKEFELLER

"I have ways of making money you know nothing about,"
Rockefeller had warned one of the Clevelanders who tried to
hold out against his juggernaut, and in fact, he did. At the time
of the Massacre, in 1872, Rockefeller controlled ten percent of
the domestic refining industry. By the start of the 1880s, Standard Oil was refining 90 percent of all the oil in the world, and
John D. Rockefeller was beginning to become very rich. There
were still, however, two variables not safely under the company's control. To be refined, oil had to come from somewhere,
and to have economic value it had to be sold somewhere. Until
Rockefeller controlled both end points of the operation, he
couldn't fully tame the market variables that affected the industry, nor could he fully maximize profits. It was time for the octopus to grow more tentacles.

To guarantee supply, the company moved backwards
through barrel making, railroad cars, and pipelines until finally
it was doing its own exploration and extrication. With supply
stabilized, Standard Oil turned next to distribution and sales.
Traditionally, oil had been sold to the market by independent
middlemen who might skim as much as five cents off the price
of a gallon of kerosene. To Rockefeller, it was both an unfor-
givable loss and an inefficient way for the company to control
and grow its sales. "We had to create selling methods far in
advance of what then existed," he would say much later. "We
had to dispose of two, or three, or four gallons of oil where one
had been sold before, and we could not rely upon the usual
trade channels then existing to accomplish this."

For starters, Rockefeller disintermediated the independents
and replaced them with his own distribution and sales force:
He had more than enough clout now to call the shots almost
at will. In their place, he provided a fleet of newly built company wagons, manned by company employees, to deliver company oil to hardware stores and markets across the country.
Where the population was dense enough, the wagons even sold

157

door to door, breaching the line between wholesale and retail, and further reinforcing the sense that all oil was Standard Oil. By the century's end, the company not only controlled nearly all domestic petroleum refining but pumped a third of America's crude oil, operated the country's second-largest steel mill, and controlled a fleet of thousands of railroad cars, barges, and ships. By then, too, it had expanded its reach into coal and iron ore.

"By the 1890s the vertical integration was complete," Jerry Useem writes in a review of Rockefeller's managerial practices for the May 1999 issue of *Inc.* magazine.

> Oil now flowed from a Standard Oil wellhead, traveled through a Standard Oil pipeline, was cleansed in a Standard Oil refinery, was shipped in a Standard Oil tank car, and was even sold at the doorstep by a Standard Oil sales agent. By internalizing each transaction in the process ("everything being within ourselves," Andrew Carnegie had called it), Standard Oil was no longer at the mercy of uncooperative suppliers, incompetent distributors, or other vagaries of the marketplace. Rockefeller had achieved order.

From that point on, the money just poured in. Over the next several decades John D. Rockefeller would amass the world's greatest fortune: At a time when most Americans were lucky to be making two dollars a day, Rockefeller was earning almost $2 a second, more than $50 million a year.

John D. Rockefeller wasn't the only man of his age to swallow his competitors and fold them all into a vertically integrated corporation capable of controlling its product with an iron first. Trust, monopolies, octopuses—call them what you will, they were all over the place. Rockefeller just did the controlling better, inventing virtually on his own a modern managerial organization to run his far-flung enterprise.

Technology helped him, certainly. By 1885, when Standard
Oil moved into its new corporate headquarters at 26 Broadway in Manhattan, the telegraph had advanced the nation's
communication network as surely as the completion of the
Transcontinental Railroad had advanced its transportation
network two decades earlier—and as surely as the Internet
would re-revolutionize communications a century later. From
his rolltop desk at Standard Oil headquarters, Rockefeller
could stay in touch with the whole enterprise he had created,
on an hourly or even more immediate basis. The danger of
micromanagement loomed. Part of Rockefeller's genius,
though, was to resist the temptation.

Instead of trying to run his business through the exercise
of his own ego or personality or through a cult of fear—and
other robber barons tried all three approaches—Rockefeller
ran Standard Oil by committee: The manufacturing committee saw to manufacturing, the purchasing committee to purchasing. Today, it sounds axiomatic to say such things; a
century ago, Rockefeller's committee system was a bold creation tailor-made for the efficient supervision of the bold enterprise he had put together by dint of a ruthless will. Rockefeller's
biographer, Ron Chernow, notes that even at executive committee meetings, where his word finally was the law, the boss
made a point of sitting mid-table, rather than at the head.

"Having created an empire of unfathomable complexity,"
Chernow writes, "he was smart enough to see that he had to
submerge his identity in the organization." And smart enough,
too, to realize that he had loosed upon the world something it
had hitherto not known, what business historian Alfred D.
Chandler Jr. has called "a new subspecies of economic man—
the salaried manager." Between 1880 and 1920—roughly the
time span of John D. Rockefeller's ultimate ascendance and
global domination—the number of professional managers in
the United States soared more than sixfold, from 161,000 to

more than a million, according to the Brookings Institution. To meet the rising demand, in 1898 the University of Chicago and the University of California both launched another new subspecies, this one of education: the business school. By the start of the new century, New York University and Dartmouth were both in the business-education business. The Harvard Business School opened its doors in 1908.

Standard Oil, Rockefeller said late in life, had been "the origin of the whole system of economic administration. It has revolutionized the way of doing business all over the world." Beyond doubt, he was right, but as he frequently did in his later years, Rockefeller was also sanitizing a good many unsavory moments along the way. In a remarkable series of interviews undertaken between 1917 and 1920 with New York news-paperman William Inglis, Rockefeller offered a point by point rebuttal to virtually every accusation leveled against him and Standard Oil by his critics, especially Ida Tarbell. Whether the interviews were ever meant to be seen—they were never aired until 60 years after his death—or were meant simply to ease Rockefeller's conscience and prepare him for his maker is unclear. Either way, they paint a history often at odds with fact. It's not by accident, one suspects, that when Nelson Rockefeller asked to interview his grandfather for a Dartmouth senior the-sis meant to vindicate the Mephistopheles of Cleveland, grand-father sent back word that he'd just as soon not. How hard it would have been for him to lie to a grandson who shared his birthday.

⁓

John D. Rockefeller was fond of noting that the law seemed to be applied ex post facto to his person and his business. The secret railroad deal that led to the Cleveland Massacre was, after all, not illegal at the time, although the courts would soon rule against it. Railroad rebates in general only became illegal

160

with the creation of the Interstate Commerce Commission in 1887, and combinations in restraint of trade—the lifeblood of vertically integrated trusts and octopuses—weren't outlawed until the Sherman Antitrust Act of 1890.

In fact, though, both Rockefeller and Standard Oil frequently operated on the fringes—or even just over the fringes—of the law. In researching his biography, Ron Chernow found numerous instances in Rockefeller's correspondence where he was simply paying off politicians to affect the outcome of legislation. The $250,000 to the 1896 McKinley campaign was only the most dramatic example of a practice Rockefeller seems to have regarded as a necessary business expense. Nor did the Interstate Commerce Commission or the Sherman Antitrust Act necessarily affect Rockefeller's behavior. Rather, he seems to have redoubled his efforts to get around the legal annoyances imposed upon his company, and in Henry Flagler and John D. Archibald, he had powerful lieutenants even less troubled by the fine points of the law and ethics than he was.

In his own lifetime, the muckrakers Henry Demarest Lloyd and, most dramatically, Ida Tarbell assembled a damning amount of evidence of wrong and shady doings on the part of Rockefeller and Standard Oil, yet it wasn't until 1906—a year after Tarbell's *McClure's* series had concluded—that Standard Oil hired its first publicist and set out to improve its public image. In part, perhaps, Rockefeller simply misjudged the groundswell of resentment against him, the power of the press, and the determination of Teddy Roosevelt to turn him into political capital: Having paid off politicians so much of his life, Rockefeller must have had trouble imagining any other way of dealing with them. In larger part, Rockefeller was able to ignore the storm because he saw himself in service to a higher calling: Purging business of its inefficiencies was service not just to the economy but to the nation and God.

Roosevelt was gone from office, replaced by William Howard Taft, by the time the law finally caught up with John D. Rockefeller. On May 15, 1911, after 21 years, 23 volumes of evidence totaling 12,000 pages, and 11 separate trials, the last one involving 444 witnesses, the U.S. Supreme Court ruled that the Standard Oil trust was indeed a monopoly and ordered the company broken up. The news reached Rockefeller on a golf course. His only response was to tell his golfing partners to buy stock in Standard Oil. It was among the sagest pieces of advice he was ever to give.

Standard Oil would be broken into 34 separate companies—among them the parent companies of such modern-day industry leaders as ExxonMobil, BP Amoco, Conoco, Inc., ARCO, BP America, and Cheesebrough Ponds—and J.D. Rockefeller would maintain control over each and every one of them. In 1911, when the Supreme Court decision came down, Rockefeller was worth around $300 million. Two years later, as a direct result of having been punished by the federal government, his worth had soared to $900 million. Losing the antitrust case turned out to be the greatest windfall of his career. By then, too, oil had found a new use: the automobile.

Not only was John D. Rockefeller made far richer by the Supreme Court decision; he also seems to have been unrepentant about it. When some twenty thousand strikers were evicted from their company-owned homes at a Rockefeller-controlled coal mine in 1913, the state militia moved in, machine-gunned the strikers and set fire to the tent colony where they had taken refuge. More than a dozen women and children died in the blaze—the infamous "Ludlow Massacre." Echoing his father's sentiments, John D. Jr. blamed the strikers for the violence, for "recklessly" insisting on their right to a union.

How much money was $900 million in 1913? Somewhere in excess of $13 billion in current dollars, but as Ron Chernow points out, focusing on that number is only one way to look at the story. The entire federal budget for the year 1913 amounted to just $715 million, nearly $200 million less than one citizen's net worth. The federal debt then was $1.2 billion; Rockefeller could have retired three-quarters of that as well. Maybe most tellingly, Rockefeller's wealth equaled about 2.5 percent of the gross national product. Judged by the same measure, the net worth of the man most recently pursued by the federal government for antitrust violations, Bill Gates, is only about one-fifth of that, but Gates, in his defense, has been allowed to keep less of his earnings. Rockefeller turned 70 years old four days before Congress proposed the Sixteenth Amendment to the Constitution, granting the government the power to levy an income tax.

Rockefeller once estimated that had he kept all the money he gave away, he would have been three times richer than he was, and trained to bookkeeping, he had a fine mind for figures. But the issue would seem to be academic at best: With John D. Rockefeller, getting and giving seem to have been two sides of the same gold coin.

9

HENRY FORD

Building Cars
and the Markets for Them

REAT FORTUNES ARE THE TRAILING INDICATOR OF great industries, and as the twentieth century dawned, America's great fortunes had been built mostly on iron and steel, railroads, and oil. Andrew Carnegie was 12 years old when his family emigrated to western Pennsylvania from Scotland. Over the next six years, Carnegie would work as a bobbin boy in a cotton factory, an engine tender, and a telegraph messenger and operator before taking a job, at age 18, with the Pennsylvania Railroad. By the late 1860s, still in his 30s, Carnegie started making the steel from which the railroad cars were made, and by 1888 he controlled, in addition to his steel mills, coal and iron stocks to feed them, plus more than four hundred miles of track and a fleet of steamships to connect the two. The next year, Carnegie published his famous essay, "The Gospel of Wealth," in which he argued that the first half of a rich man's life should be devoted to making money and the second half to giving it away in a manner that most benefited the commonwealth. A dozen years later, in 1901, a syndicate organized by J.P. Morgan bought out Carnegie and consolidated his holdings into the U.S. Steel Company, and Andrew Carnegie, who pocketed $240 million in the deal, set out to distribute his fortune, most notably by providing public libraries throughout the United States and Great Britain.

Because it never was consolidated in the same way steel was, the railroad industry created more but lesser fortunes, many of them as memorable for the underhand way they were amassed as for the generosity by which they were distributed. Collis Huntington, Leland Stanford, and the others who profited mightily from the completion of the Transcontinental Railroad were only representative of their breed. Jay Gould and James Fisk were masters of flooding the market with fraudulent stock to protect their rail interests. Cornelius Vanderbilt, who started out in the shipping business before switching his interests to trains, would lose millions battling Gould and Fisk for the Erie Railway. Vanderbilt still managed to amass an estate in the range of $100 million before his death in 1877, but his major bequest—$1 million to endow Vanderbilt University in Nashville, Tennessee—seems puny by comparison to Carnegie's largess.

Oil, of course, gave industry its greatest and one of its most ruthless consolidators and both the richest man of his day and the most generous: John D. Rockefeller. To produce history's first billionaire, though, would require the intersection of three things: a new invention that could do what the railroads couldn't do—let people go wherever they had a mind to travel, whenever they had a mind to go there; a nation built on the aesthetic of wide open spaces; and a man smart enough to marry mass production to mass consumption and to help provide the means for both. Horseless carriages would make the steel barons and Rockefellers richer still: They were made mostly of steel, after all, and they opened up a vast new market for Standard Oil and its refined petroleum. But the automobile would make Henry Ford richer than them all.

⟨≋⟩

Self-propulsion is a dream as old as mankind, but it had also been a reality—if not a terribly practical one—for more than two centuries before Henry Ford unleashed his "Tin Lizzie" on the American public. A model steam carriage built by a Jesuit missionary had been demonstrated successfully in China in the late seventeenth century. Nearly a hundred years earlier, two-masted, wind-propelled land "ships" in Holland were maintaining speeds of 20 miles an hour with up to 28 passengers on board, so long as the weather cooperated. The eighteenth century saw successful experimentation in wound-spring engines (the clock method) and others powered by compressed air. The first forerunner of the modern auto would seem to be a steam-powered tricycle built by the Frenchman Nicholas Joseph Cugnot, and an imposing invention it truly was: A 1769 version capable of carrying four people ran for 20 minutes at 2.25 miles an hour. The four-stroke engine, a direct ancestor of today's internal combustion engines, was the brainchild of another Frenchman, Alphonse Beau de Rochas. Two German inventors, Gottlieb Daimler and Carl Benz, generally get credit for refining the gasoline-powered engine to a point where commercial production was feasible. Benz sold his first car to a Parisian in 1887. A few years later, Daimler got into the business. (Although the two men never met, their firms would be merged in 1926 into Daimler-Benz, manufacturers of the famous Mercedes-Benz line.)

If Europe gets credit for the technical innovations that launched the auto industry, it was in the United States that the industry caught hold and flourished. Europe had more people, but by dint of its geography, the United States had the greater need—and by the start of the twentieth century it also had the native capital to support the growth. Frank and Charles Duryea began installing gasoline-powered engines into old horse carriages in the early 1890s. By 1903, there were eleven thousand cars on the roads of America. The next year, in 1904, Ransom Olds added 5,000 more with his 3-horsepower Oldsmobiles and proved that it was possible to make a handsome living in the automobile trade. Beginning in 1903 and extended over the next 5 years, a full 20 dozen auto-manufacturing firms went into business in the United States, including one founded by a backyard Michigan inventor named Henry Ford.

Until Henry Ford came along, the automobile belonged to those rich enough to afford one: Ransom Olds' earliest 1900 models sold for $1,250, more than a hundred times the weekly wage of the average factory worker. Ford, though, had a different vision. Sell a car cheaply enough, and you'll create a market demand. Create a market demand, and the margin you fail to make on unit sales will be made back many times over on volume. Do all that, and instead of being a play thing of the rich, the automobile will become a necessity of the American Everyman.

In 1908, the Ford Motor Company began producing the Model T—faster than a horse, sturdy enough to withstand America's primitive roads, unremarkable as to its parts and looks, but at $825 closer to affordable for the working Joe— and both car and vision ran like a dream. Ford sold more than ten thousand Model T's in its first year of production, bringing in more than $9 million to a company that had been capitalized with $28,000 only 5 years earlier and had set up shop with a dozen workmen in a plant all of 250 feet by 50 feet.

⟿

Born on a farm near Dearborn, Michigan, in 1863 and educated in one-room school houses, Henry Ford was barely able to handle his McGuffey reader when he quit formal education for good at age 15, but he was an ace at mathematics and he loved machinery. Ford was 16 years old when he walked to

Detroit to take a job as an apprentice engineer, a position he was fired from in less than a week. Undaunted, he moved on to a job repairing watches and another working on ship engines, two skills he would never forget. Decades later—a billionaire and a global figure—Ford still took delight in taking apart and reassembling his friends' pocket watches and in occasionally getting down on the factory floor with one of his greasy engines.

Automobiles, though, not watches or ship engines caught Henry Ford's greatest attention. A little after midnight on June 4, 1896, he finished building his first experimental car in a brick shed behind the duplex where he and his wife, Clara, were living. Dubbed a "Quadricycle" and a scant five hundred pounds in weight, the car ran on four bicycle tires. Three years later, he successfully demonstrated a second prototype by driving it roundtrip from Detroit to Pontiac, Michigan, and soon formed his first business, the Detroit Automobile Company, with $15,000 raised from a dozen shareholders. The company would last two years, during which time time Ford managed to build less than two dozen cars—but his reputation in the nascent auto industry didn't suffer. By 1903, Ford had established himself as the premier designer of American racing cars and formed the Ford Motor Company.

Like nearly all other auto manufacturers of the time, Ford manufactured almost nothing. Chassis and engines both came from a machine shop run by two of his minority shareholders, Horace and John Dodge. Ford simply assembled the parts into a finished product. In 1905, though, Ford would take a first critical step toward separating his company from the teeming multitude. Other auto makers created, at best, loose associations with dealers and left servicing up to the inventiveness of locals. The Ford Motor Company was barely two years old before it had factory-trained mechanics in the field. Simultaneously, Ford was working to bring the entire product under one roof. By

1912, the company was making its own crankcases, axles, and other critical parts. The next year, Ford bought out the Dodge brothers' interest in his company and began manufacturing his own engines and finished chassis as well. Now he could direct his attention not only to the product but to the entire means of production. Already on his way to being super rich, Henry Ford was about to become super famous.

Like the automobile itself, the principles of the assembly line were far from new by the time Ford came around to them. The French army had been experimenting with standardized musket parts even before the American Revolution. The year the revolution began, the Englishman Jeremiah Wilkinson had come up with the jig, which allowed workers to make identical parts in series. Ford himself would credit the inspiration for the assembly line to Chicago meat packers and the overhead trolley they used to carry carcasses along a line while butchers, in effect, disassembled them. Ford simply took existing principles and married them to necessity. By the early 1910s, his motor company had very nearly wrung the maximum potential out of traditional production methods. If he was going to create a true mass market for his automobiles, he would need to mass manufacture them, and that meant the assembly line. Ford never doubted that he could sell cars as fast as his people could make them. Production speed was the challenge. Solve that, and the mass market would take care of itself.

In his 1922 autobiography *My Life & Work*, one of three that Ford would collaborate on during his life, he described how the first automobile assembly line came to be. Initially, he wrote, a Ford car had been assembled "in exactly the same way one builds a house."

"We simply started to put a car together at a spot on the floor and workmen brought to it the parts as they were needed ... [but] the rapid press of production made it necessary to devise plans of production that would avoid having the workers falling over one another." To do that, Ford went on, "we began taking the work to the men instead of the men to the work. We now have two general principles in all operations—that a man shall never have to take more than one step, if possibly it can be avoided, and that no man need ever stoop over."

The principles of assembly are these:

1. Place the tools and the men in the sequence of the operation so that each component part shall travel the least possible distance while in the process of finishing.

2. Use work slides or some other form of carrier so that when a workman completes his operation, he drops the part always in the same place—which place must always be the most convenient place to his hand—and if possible have gravity carry the part to the next workman for his operation.

3. Use sliding assembling lines by which the parts to be assembled are delivered at convenient distances.

The net result of the application of these principles is the reduction of the necessity for thought on the part of the worker and the reduction of his movements to a minimum. He does as nearly as possible only one thing with only one movement.

Ford had already built and put into operation the most modern factory in the automobile industry—the well-lit and well-ventilated Highland Park plant, which opened in early 1910. There, in April 1913, he launched his first experiment in assembly-line production, beginning with the flywheel magneto. (A magneto uses magnets to generate electricity in an internal-combustion engine.) Previously the job had been performed by a single worker who turned out magnetos at the rate of about one every twenty minutes. Now the same job was spread into 29 assembly line operations, with the result that average assembly time was cut by more than a third, to 13 minutes 10 seconds. A year later, the company raised the height of the assembly line 8 inches; this time, the average production time was lowered to 7 minutes. Further experimentation brought the time down to 5 minutes.

Simultaneously, the principles applied to the magneto were being applied to the engine as a whole. Instead of one man assembling an entire motor from start to finish, the work was split into 84 operations and productivity was raised threefold. Soon, the experimentation with parts of the production process was spreading to the process as a whole. Within months of full assembly-line production, the time needed to turn out a Model T had been cut from over 12 hours to under 2. By sweeping up the sawdust, metal shavings, and coke dust from the factory floors and feeding them to the steam-power plant, Ford found that he could save another $600,000 a year in fuel costs. With production costs slashed dramatically, Ford slashed the price of the car—nearly twenty years after it was first produced, a Model T coupe would be selling for less than a third of what it had originally cost. As the price dropped, sales quadrupled: By the end of 1914, almost half of all cars sold in America were Henry Ford's Model T's.

"Time loves to be wasted," Ford had fumed back in the days when it seemed to take forever to turn out his automobiles. Now he was telling reporters that mass production was the "new messiah." As if to prove the practical application of his words, Henry and Clara Ford moved into "Fair Lane," a 2,000-acre estate near where he had been born—their eleventh address in 23 years of marriage. Secure in his leadership of America's next great industry and ensconced at last in a mansion worthy of his greatness, Ford proclaimed to the *Chicago Tribune's* Charles Wheeler that "History is more or less bunk.... The only history that is worth a tinker's damn is the history we make today." Before he could turn the world industrial order completely on its ear, though, Henry Ford would have to solve his labor problems.

The executives of the Ford Motor Company and their beancounters loved the assembly line and the economies of scale it created. Ford's workers, though, had a different take on the process. "The reduction of his movements to a minimum" that Henry Ford wrote about must have pleased many of them, but "the reduction of the necessity for thought on the part of the worker" was very nearly insulting.

Even before the assembly line, Ford had been bothered by a high labor turnover: The company's productivity demands were among the most stringent in the business. With the coming of mass production—known originally as "Fordism"—the labor turnover turned into a near plague. By the close of 1913, Ford had to hire nearly a thousand people every time it wanted to find another hundred permanent workers, and such was the success of its cars that it needed to expand the work force almost constantly.

To solve the problem and to thwart a unionization drive launched in the summer of 1913 by the Industrial Workers of the World, in 1914 Henry Ford introduced what was to be his second great industrial innovation: a $5 wage for an eight-hour day, about 15 percent more than the prevailing rate in the auto industry and well more than double the average manufacturing wage nationwide, for what was often a shorter day's work.

"In underpaying men," Ford would say, "we are preparing a generation of underfed children who will be physically and morally undernourished; we will have a generation of workers weak in body and spirit who, for this reason, will be inefficient when they come into industry. It is industry who will foot the bill."

The rhetoric was high-blown, as it often was with Ford, but the calculation was cold-blooded as well. Instead of a revolving employment door, the company now had men lined up for work; and it had a work force that, with diligence and thrift, could afford the product they were manufacturing. "Purchasers," Ford once explained, "are made, not born."

The five-dollar-day, Ford was later to write, "was one of the finest cost-cutting moves we ever made." Better still, from Ford's point of view, it gave him even more control over his workers. Within days of introducing the new pay scale, Ford fired up to nine hundred Greek and Russian Orthodox employees who had stayed away from work to celebrate Christmas on the day designated by the Julian calendar, according to their tradition. To the rest of the company's workers, the message was simple and clear: Extra pay would demand extra and greater allegiance.

To assure that its flow-production system ran unimpeded, the company restricted workers to a single 15-minute lunch break, including restroom time. On the job, men were forbidden to lean on machines, sit, squat, whistle, talk, or smoke. To make sure they complied, company "spotters" patrolled the factory floor. Soon workers were learning to communicate without moving their lips, a form of ventriloquism that became enshrined as the "Ford whisper." To avoid alerting prowling straw bosses, workers developed frozen expressions that came to be known as the "Fordization" of the face.

Neither Henry Ford nor his company stopped at the factory floor. Productive labor required a proper home environment and decent habits, and the $5 a day wage gave Ford and his men the entree to attack both. Officially called a "profit sharing arrangement," the wage plan split compensation into a base hourly rate of 34 cents an hour—or $2.72 for an 8-hour day—and an additional "profit-sharing" rate of 28.5 cents an hour. To qualify for the latter, workers had to perform satisfactorily both on and off the production line, and that meant meeting human quality standards as strict and as strictly enforced as the standards imposed on automobiles.

Ford promulgated a series of rules meant to assure that its employees were not just good workers but what it considered good citizens. Workers were expected to show thrift, to live in a proper house (in particular, a house that didn't take in boarders), to have no outside sources of income (including a working wife), to not associate with nor allow their children to associate with the wrong kind of people (union sympathizers and organizers most notably), to show progress toward learning English in the case of immigrant laborers, to neither drink nor smoke excessively, to avoid gambling, and to be guilty of no "malicious practice derogatory to good physical manhood or moral character." Through its newly created Sociological Department, Ford sent counselors out to advise workers and the families on how best to meet the requirements that would qualify them for the profit-sharing bonus; on the side, the counselors acted as spies, reporting back on those who seemed to be falling away from the secular faith.

About two in five Ford workers were disqualified from the plan in its early months; if they failed to mend their way within half a year, they were let go and their escrowed profit share was donated to charity. Within two years, the disqualification ratio had shrunk to about one in four, but the extra money they received for compliance was rapidly shrinking in value. By 1918, wartime inflation had brought the buying power of Ford's $5 day down to $2.80 in 1914 dollars, and Henry Ford himself was worrying less about the moral content of his work force than about union activity in his factories. The Socialization Department—later renamed the Education Department—was disbanded in 1921 and its records were burned. In its place arose the Ford Service Department, thugs and labor-spies under the leadership of an ex-boxer named Harry Bennett, charged with keeping Ford an open shop.

By then, too, Henry Ford could call the shots any way he wanted to. Ford succeeded in buying out the last non-family stockholders in 1919. As the 1920s began, he sat atop a tightly held, vertically integrated industrial behemoth with main plants at Highland Park and River Rouge; branch plants around the world, including assembly plants in Canada and England, iron mines and lumber mills, Brazilian rubber plantations, glass manufacturers, and a railroad, and fleet of ships to move the cars to markets anywhere. Possessed of almost infinite wealth and power—no man in the world had ever held in one grip so much industrial might—Ford now set out to become a prophet as well.

Fifty years earlier, J.P. Morgan had overseen the massive transfer of European capital to the United States. By the early 1920s, through his books and frequent interviews, Ford began to export back to Europe an entire philosophy of doing business. Labor should be rationalized through mechanization, work should be divided and specialized, and workers bought off with high wages to perform the dull, repetitious tasks expected of them. Production management needed to be centralized, control needed to be hierarchical, and corporations should be vertically integrated wherever possible, employing a circle of subcontractors to help stabilize inevitable cyclical demand. Standardization and mass production meant lower costs, and lower costs meant greater profits. To protect all of the above, unionization needed to be fought with every available tool. Collectively, these and other tenets of the Fordist philosophy came to represent the new industrial order that would dominate corporate thinking for the better part of the century.

Henry Ford was no less quiet in his views on broader international affairs. An outspoken opponent of America's entry into World War I, he once promised to spend half his fortune if it could shorten the war by a single day. More practically, but perhaps only slightly more so, he set sail for Europe in late 1915 aboard a Ford-sponsored "Peace Ship" bound for Scandinavia and the Netherlands with technical advisers, delegates to a peace conference, and a largely skeptical press pool. When Ford became sick and had to lay up in Oslo, the mission fell apart.

Back home, he formed a trade school and donated money to build a hospital, both named after him. He dabbled with educational theory as well, set up a series of rural shops where farmers could produce auto parts using water power, and threw his support behind a variety of "wholesome" undertakings, from square dancing to discouraging meat consumption in favor of soybean meal. All of it made news because no one in American business, then or since, has been so large a national figure.

Ford ran for the United States Senate in 1918, as a Democrat in Republican-dominated Michigan, losing by less than five thousand votes. By 1920, Ford for President clubs were springing up across the nation. Whatever the reality of Ford's $5 a day wage and whatever the truth of everyday life inside and outside the factory for a Ford employee, Ford's brand of welfare capitalism was magic with the public: Ford was seen as another Great Emancipator, a Lincoln of the working man. A nationwide poll for *Collier's Weekly* magazine in the summer of 1923 found Ford running far ahead of the sitting president, Warren Harding. The presidential boom ended when Ford announced in October 1924 that he would back Calvin Coolidge, who had succeeded to the presidency upon Harding's death, but Ford's popularity was barely diminished. In 1926, he announced the establishment of a radical five-day work week for his employees. Three years later, in late November 1929 with a cancer sweeping through the economy, Ford responded to a Herbert Hoover request not to lower wages by actually raising them—to $7 a day. Typically in both cases, he accompanied the grand gesture with draconian cuts: As many as thirty thousand Ford workers were let go on the eve of his new "depression-beating wage," and those that remained were required to fulfill production quotas nearly 50 percent higher than the pre-salary-boost quotas. By the late 1920s, though, Ford had more to worry about than his public approval ratings: After nearly two decades of dominating the auto business as few figures have ever dominated a major industry, Henry Ford finally had to acknowledge that Alfred Sloan and his General Motors were about to eat his lunch.

The Model T wasn't the first car Henry Ford produced: Models A, B, C, F, K, N, R, and S preceded it, some of them fairly expensive as Ford searched for the right marriage of product and market demand. But for a long time it seemed as if the Model T might be the last car the Ford Motor Company ever made. Behind Ford's obstinance lay both a philosophy and a rock-hard commitment: If you keep the model static while constantly improving and refining production methods, the unit cost will continuously fall, and the product will sell itself. Sloan had a different philosophy: Flood the market with a car for every price range, change the models marginally every year and substantially every three years, and spend millions of dollars on advertising to create consumer demand, and the public will beat a path to your door. By 1927, there was no denying that Sloan and GM were on to something.

In 1921, Ford had outsold GM's bottom-of-the-line Chevrolet—the closest competitor to the Model T—by a 13 to 1 margin, but as the 1920s wore on, demand for automobiles shifted from first-time purchases to replacement cars, and as that happened, auto buyers began weighing comfort, style, and mechanical innovation. Ford was still offering a bare-bones car built for rough turn-of-the-century roads, and he was still counting on the Ford name to bring buyers in. Under the leadership of former Ford executive William Knudsen, Chevrolet meanwhile had been retooled and redesigned. Heavily promoted through ads, Chevrolet steadily closed the gap with Ford until by 1926 one Chevy was selling for every two Model Ts. The next year, on May 27, 1927, Model T production was halted and Ford plants closed while a successor was designed and the factories retooled to produce it. A little more than six months later, on December 2, 1927, the Model A was introduced.

To promote its new model, Ford spent more in one week on advertising than the company had spent collectively over the 19-year lifespan of the Model T. (Thanks to the sale of more than fifteen million Model Ts during that time and to its own stringent financial practices, Ford Motor Company had some $700 million in surplus cash with which to launch the Model A.) The campaign worked—Ford recaptured the lead from GM in total car sales—but for the rest of his life, Ford would resent the necessity of advertising.

"We are no longer in the automobile business," he once grumbled. In the auto industry as elsewhere, image was becoming everything, and Ford's own image was fading fast.

~~~

"Ford talks like a Socialist," one Wall Street operator had complained to another in a popular joke of the mid-1920s. "Yes," the other answered, "but he acts like one of us, and he gets away with it." As the Roaring '20s limped into the Depressed '30s, though, the dual nature of the great auto maker was becoming more apparent, and his difficult aspects far harder to ignore.

On the labor front, Ford's increasingly violent reactions to attempts at union organization began to run against the new spirit of the times. During the March 1932 Ford Hunger March by union-minded Ford workers, Dearborn, Michigan, police fired at point-blank range on the demonstrators, killing 3 and wounding 50, including a *New York Times* photographer shot in the head. Ten years earlier, the public might have been tempted to look the other way. By 1932, though, deprivation was everywhere, and the public was becoming more aware of the price Ford workers had had to pay for the "New Prosperity" that had been visited upon them. Henry Ford "is hated by nearly everyone who has ever worked for him, and at one time was worshipped by nearly everyone who has not," the social critic Jonathan Leonard wrote that year. Note the phrase "at one time."

Ford's reemergence as the auto sales leader was only temporary as well. For all the hullabaloo that surrounded the Model A's arrival, it was highly conventional car in both its looks and its machinery. Technically, the company would take another gigantic stride in 1932 when it introduced the Model 18 V-8, with its single-unit cast engine block, the prototype for decades of engines to follow, but Ford and its founder had missed a larger message: Even in hard times, buyers were interested in style, comfort, and convenience.

Internationally, Henry Ford was to become even harder to justify, or swallow, as the 1930s went along. The *Dearborn Independent*, a magazine backed financially by Ford and edited by William Cameron, was among the most vitriolic of the anti-Semitic tracts that sprang up in America after World War I, and one of the most insistent at publicizing the scurrilous, Russian-born, anti-Jewish tract *The Protocols of the Elders of Zion*. Ford's own contributions to the Dearborn magazine were collected into the book *The International Jew*, which, like *The Protocols*, charged Jews with plotting the destruction of Christian civilization. Across the ocean, Ford found increasing favor with the leader of Germany's National Socialist Party and his minions. The leader of the Hitler youth movement would testify after the war that he learned to hate Jews not from the rantings of Adolph Hitler but from the writings of Henry Ford. Ford is also the only American to win plaudits in Hitler's *Mein Kampf*. To underscore his admiration, Hitler sent his own thanks along with the Third Reich's Grand Cross of the Supreme Order of the German Eagle to the automaker on the occasion of his 75th birthday, in July 1938, and Ford was glad to receive both. Addled by a severe stroke earlier that year, he

had become convinced that Franklin Roosevelt was a war merchant controlled by GM and the Duponts.

Not nearly so generous in his life as John D. Rockefeller and
Andrew Carnegie had been, Henry Ford in death would give
away billions of dollars through the Ford Foundation, and the
Foundation itself would save his heirs over $300 million in fed-
eral inheritance taxes. In time, too, the Foundation's generous
support of a variety of liberal and social-welfare programs—
causes Ford himself might well have loathed—would help buff
the image of the automaker and rescue him from the consequences of many of the actions of his later years. And therein
might lie the final irony of a very conflicted and conflicting life:
A product, Henry Ford always felt, should be able to sell itself.

10

ROBERT WOODRUFF

The Brand's the Thing

T HE INDUSTRIAL REVOLUTION CREATED WHAT HAD never existed before in such profusion in human history: a multiplicity of products, designed to do almost everything and serve almost every need. The companion Consumer Revolution created something new as well: a mass market of multiple wants and needs. Increasingly, as the nineteenth century spilled over into the twentieth one, the media became the medium between the two.

Between 1830 and the start of the Civil War, the number of magazines and newspapers in circulation in the United States grew sixfold, to more than five thousand titles. Literacy was on the rise, along with the population. If the war brought severe deprivation to the South—even buttons and nails became precious commodities as the fighting wore on—in the North it stimulated economic growth and introduced new sources of raw materials. With the Union restored, war production was converted to the production of consumer goods, and as that happened, the modern print advertisement was born.

Suddenly, every product had a slogan; every slogan sought to influence choice; and the more choice there was, the greater the need to exert influence over it became. The combination, needless to say, was a publisher's best friend. In 1867 advertising expenditures of all sorts reached about $50 million in the United States. Thirteen years later, by 1880, that figure was climbing past $200 million, and by 1900 it had topped half a billion dollars. By the end of the nineteenth century, popular monthlies like *Cosmopolitan* and *McClure's* were running a hundred pages of ads in a single issue. Two decades later, a new advertising medium, radio, would blanket the nation just as choice had moved into overdrive. Radio attracted over $10 million in ads in 1928; in 1929, total ad expenditures for all media outlets approached $3.5 billion.

By then, too, the advertising industry had found one of its most messianic practitioners—a man who was to be the most successful brand-builder of the twentieth century. A college dropout, he would take a product manufactured of colored and sugared water, virtually indistinguishable from its competitors, and turn it by sheer marketing and organizational genius into the most successful global product the world has ever known. His name was Robert Woodruff. His product was Coca-Cola. And here's one tangible measure of his success: The Coca-Cola Company went public in 1928 at $40 a share, 5 years after Woodruff had taken over a moribund 40-year-old business. Seven decades later, in 1998, one of those original $40 shares, assuming all dividends had been reinvested, had grown to $6.8 million, an annualized rate of return of about 25 percent. Possessed of a considerable amount of those original shares himself, Robert Woodruff enjoyed the ride. By the time of his death, in 1985 at age 95, Woodruff had donated a total of $200 million to the school he dropped out of in 1909: Emory University.

⤙

Little about Robert Woodruff's childhood augured great success. Born into a wealthy Atlanta household, Woodruff and his two younger brothers suffered under the iron fist of a domineering, puritanical father who appears to have banned fun from the home. A poor student and never an intellectual—his underlings at Coca-Cola would wonder years later if he had ever finished a book—Woodruff flunked out of Boys' High School and was sent off to Georgia Military Academy to finish his secondary schooling. He fared no better there as a student and showed no greater inclination to concentrate in or out of the classroom, but at his father's insistence he entered Emory, then a college located in Oxford, Georgia, in the fall of 1908. He was to last there one semester. "I do not think it advisable for him to return to college this term," the Emory president wrote Woodruff's father. "He has never learned to apply himself, which together with very frequent absences, makes it impossible for him to succeed as a student."

At age 19, Robert Woodruff found himself shoveling sand for the General Pipe and Foundry Company, a mostly uneducated laborer, going nowhere in a hurry. Fourteen years later, when the 33-year-old Woodruff was offered the presidency of Coca-Cola at $36,000 a year, he was already earning $75,000 annually and had a $250,000-a-year offer on the table to become president of Standard Oil. What happened in between? Life proved a better educator than schools, and a better forum for finding success.

After knocking around in a succession of jobs including purchasing agent for an ice company, Woodruff landed a position through an Atlanta acquaintance as southeastern salesman for the White Motor Company, and there he learned that, whatever his faults as a student, he could sell almost anything to almost anybody. Direct and honest in his dealings, Woodruff developed an unerring instinct for what he called "the man of consequence," the one who could close the deal. Born to the manor if not exactly raised that way, he also possessed a confidence and comfort in dealing with top brass that many of his competitors lacked.

Woodruff left White for the duration of World War I to serve in the U.S. Ordnance Department, but he didn't neglect his former and future employer: A troop transport truck he helped develop added significantly to White's bottom line during the war years. Nor did Woodruff's success or his abilities go unnoticed by his disapproving father. When Ernest Woodruff put together a syndicate to buy the Coca-Cola Company in 1919 for $25 million, he offered his son a chance to get in on the ground floor, which he did at $5 a share in the private offering. (Woodruff also made sure that his hunting pal, the "Georgia Peach" Ty Cobb, got in on the action as well, an act of friendship that feathered Cobb's nest luxuriously in his later years.) And when the management of the company they had bought proved unable to meet expectations, Ernest Woodruff and his syndicate partners again called on Robert, this time to point the soft-drink maker in the right direction.

As an Atlantan, Woodruff knew the product well. Coca-Cola had been around since 1886 when a local patent-medicine blender named John Stith Pemberton had concocted its caramel-colored syrup in a three-legged brass kettle in his own backyard. As a Methodist, Woodruff might have known Coke even better. His Sunday school teacher growing up was Asa Candler, the Atlanta entrepreneur who bought the company in 1891 for $2,300 and took the soft drink nationwide four years later. About the soft-drink business itself, Woodruff cheerfully acknowledged that he didn't know anything more "than a pig knows about Sunday." But as a salesman he surely knew the biggest obstacle facing him: At White Motors, he had been offering up a product with a clear utility—trucks move things, they connect markets and customers. At Coca-Cola, Woodruff would be offering for sale a product that absolutely no one needed.

Robert Woodruff deserves credit for far more than the brilliant ad campaigns he so insisted on. Difficult in many

ways as a boss—he hated to be alone, and would often call
his executives at the last moment to come for dinner or
because he was awake in the middle of the night—Woodruff
was nonetheless a talent picker par excellence. The ranks of
his top aides were filled with former Georgia Tech football
players in whom Woodruff had spotted business potential and
with one-time opponents whom he converted to allies, including Arthur Acklin, an IRS agent who had come to Woodruff's
attention when he was trying to dun Coca-Cola for back
taxes.

Where taxes were the issue, Woodruff also could play hard-
ball with the best of them. When Georgia governor Eugene
Talmadge tried to impose a Depression-era business tax that
would have cut into Coca-Cola's profits, Woodruff reincorpo-
rated the company and moved its administrative headquarters
to Wilmington, Delaware. For a decade, until the Georgia legislature backed off the tax, Coke—the quintessential Atlanta
company—wasn't really that at all.

Like other corporations in the increasingly science-minded
1920s, Coca-Cola under Woodruff embraced surveying and
market research. Few other companies, though, gave themselves over so thoroughly to the results. Beginning in 1927,
Mark Pendergrast writes in his thorough and entertaining history of the company, *For God, Country & Coca-Cola*, the company's field researchers spent three years analyzing fifteen
thousand retail outlets to determine the exact ratio between
sales volume and traffic flow, so that sales teams would know
nearly to the minute how much attention to lavish on each spot
where Coke was sold. They followed that up with a survey of
forty-two thousand soda-fountain customers to track the
relationship between initial purchase of the product and a
follow-up choice of Coke.

Woodruff applied the principles of science internally as
well. Under Asa Candler and his relations, Coca-Cola had run

less by dictate than by instinct. Under Woodruff, there were rules and procedure manuals for everything, from bookkeeping practices to the servicing of dispensers, the color of trucks, the uniforms worn by the drivers, the way a Coca-Cola was poured at the soda fountain, and the presentation and punctuation of the trademark logo. (The name and logo themselves had been the work of John Pemberton's bookkeeper, Frank Robinson, who thought the two uppercase *Cs* would look good in ads.) Coke's bottlers were historically an independent lot, but even there Woodruff did his best to bring order and predictability. Coke lore is resplendent with tales of his efforts, including the story about Woodruff's visit to a particularly filthy and disreputable looking bottling plant.

"The Boss summoned the owner and told him he'd better clean up his operation by the next day, or he would soon find himself in some other line of work," Mark Pendergrast recounts.

" 'But Mr. Woodruff,' the bottler protested, 'it don't do no good to clean up. The next day it'll just look like this again.' There was a moment of tense silence as Woodruff slowly and deliberately took his cigar out of his mouth, his eyes boring holes into the bottler. 'You wipe your ass, don't you?' Woodruff said. With that, he replaced the cigar and left. . . ."

Apocryphal? Quite possibly, but one suspects that Woodruff and his inner circle would have happily encouraged the legend. Better than anyone else of their generation, they understood the importance of brand, and they understood that brand gets built both externally, through customer interaction with the product and its messages, and internally, through the myths a company tells itself about itself.

Most of all, though, Robert Woodruff understood that brand gets built through advertising, and not just any advertising.

By the 1920s negative advertising had become very nearly the standard of the industry. Domestic tragedy waited around every corner, and lapses in personal hygiene had far-reaching consequences. The wrong hand cream, the wrong detergent, or stockings, or foodstuff could cost you your job, your social standing, your friends, your health, or even a future for your children. Postum sold its caffeine-free, grain-based hot breakfast beverage not by promoting its taste but by showing a boy "Held Back by Coffee" who was being tutored after school to make up for his academic deficiencies. Hoover sold its vacuum cleaners not through promises of cleanliness but by screaming in print that "Dirty Rugs Are Dangerous!" Ads that weren't negatively on the offense were positively on the defense, trying to counter the charges made against their products.

In the years before Woodruff took over the company, Coca-Cola had gone down both paths. One standard ad for the product showed a relentless sun beating down on shoppers: Buy Coke or melt, seemed to be the message. Another featured the testimony of a Dr. Schmiedeberg that Coca-Cola was, indeed, not addictive or ruinous to the brain, digestive tract, or moral fiber. ("A woman who becomes an addict to it loses her divine right to bring children into the world," United States Senator Tom Watson had assured his colleagues in 1921.) Such charges would persist throughout the 1920s, kept alive by the Women's Christian Temperance Union and by the company's use of decaffeinated coca leaves in the manufacturing process. Under Woodruff, though, and with the considerable help of Archie Lee and the D'Arcy ad agency, the tenor of the company's advertising campaigns would change entirely: Drinking a Coca-Cola wasn't a moral or political or social matter, although doing so would put you in plenty of good company. Drinking a Coke wasn't an issue of health, either, although it sure couldn't hurt you. Most of all and most important, drinking a Coke was simply a chance to do something nice for yourself, a little moment of pleasure in an all too hectic world.

Archie Lee's famous phrase "The Pause That Refreshes" didn't appear in print until 1929, in an ad that ran in the *Sat-*

urday Evening Post, but the spirit of the slogan was there before the slogan ever arrived. Coca-Cola was a way to "enjoy thirst at work or at play." It was "always delightful," a good reason to stop in a "cool and cheerful place." "Refresh Yourself," a 1924 ad advised: "The Charm of Coca-Cola Is Proclaimed at All Soda Fountains."

To drive the words home, the D'Arcy agency brought on some of the best illustrators of the day, Norman Rockwell and N.C. Wyeth among them, to create images that would tie the soft drink to the enduring moments of its customers. "You are selling not just a soft drink, but an *idea*," Woodruff told his ad people, and in Norman Rockwell's paintings of freckle-faced boys sitting by the fishing hole with a Coke and the family dog, he got just the idea he was looking for. All that was best about America was best about Coca-Cola. Rather than merely echo culture, Coke's ads began to define it. Prior to 1931, Santa Claus was variously depicted in the United States and Europe as tall and gaunt or as an elf; he dressed in anything from blue to yellow. In 1931, though, Haddon Sundblom produced the first in what would be an annual series of Christmas ads for Coca-Cola, and forever after Santa would look just as Sundblom had drawn him: fat and jolly with high black boots and a broad black belt and always dressed in Coca-Cola red.

In 1938, a D'Arcy executive spelled out for the ad agency 35 rules for Coca-Cola advertising that reflect both Woodruff's penchant for fine dicta and product micromanagement, and his broader concern for brand and image. Among the rules:

~ Never split the trade mark "Coca-Cola" in two lines.
~ When the cooler is open, the righthand side which shows the bottle opener should be opened if possible.
~ The trademark must never be obliterated so that it is not perfectly legible.

194

~ Never refer to Coca-Cola as "it."
~ Never use Coca-Cola in a personal sense—such as, "Coca-Cola invites you to lunch."
~ Never show or imply that Coca-Cola should be drunk by very young children.
~ On oil paintings or color photographs be inclined to show a brunette rather than a blond girl if one girl is in the picture.
~ Adolescent girls or young women should be the wholesome type; not sophisticated looking.

Within the D'Arcy agency, the wholesome though almost always buxom brunettes who drank Cokes in the company's ads came to be known as "the Atlanta virgins"—"sexy only above the hips," as one ad executive explained.

❧

If Coke's ads tended to celebrate an idealized world, its media campaigns and merchandising were anything but nostalgic. The history of Coca-Cola during the Woodruff years is the history of taking advantage of every new technological, cultural, and social phenomena in American life.

Six hundred thousand miles of highways were built in the 1920s—Americans were taking to the road, and Coke took to the road along with them. The first of the "Ritz boy" billboards appeared in 1925: a smiling bellhop holding a tray with a bottle of the soft drink and a glass on it. "6,000,000 a day," the caption read, reminiscent of the slogan McDonald's would employ so successfully decades later. The bottle in the Ritz boy ad was telling: Coca-Cola had been built on soda-fountain sales. By the mid-1920s it was dispensed at every one of the roughly 115,000 soda fountains in America. Now, in keeping with company policy that Coke should always be "within arm's reach of desire," Woodruff went after the 1.5 million filling stations that had sprung up along the new highways to serve the newly traveling public. That meant bottles—service station owners pumped gas, they didn't mix soft drinks—and bottles meant a new and standardized dispenser so that the motoring public would always know that a Coke was waiting inside and that the Coke would always be cold. In 1928, the company developed a square metal ice box on a stand, in Coca-Cola red, and found a manufacturer to produce it for only $12.50. Within twelve months, 32,000 of the dispenser boxes had been sold, and bottled Coca-Cola was outselling soda-fountain drinks for the first time. Five years later, the ice boxes would be replaced with an electric cooler developed by Westinghouse—competitors called them the "red devils." Soon, the electric coolers would be coin-operated, and the modern soft-drink dispenser would be born. As one bottler put it, the cooler is "advertising manager, salesman, clerk, delivery boy, warehouseman, and sometimes even the cash register all at the same time."

The bottle had given Coca-Cola legs: It could go where the market was. The six-pack would give the soft drink bulk, too. Woodruff had experimented with a Coca-Cola six pack—then known as a "six box"—in the mid-1920s, but it wasn't until the early 1930s that home refrigeration was sufficiently widespread to create a market. Then, the company pounced. Almost overnight, its new boxes could be bought in thousands of A & P and Piggly Wiggly food stores. To push the market, Coke employed a small army of women to go door to door, handing out coupons for free samples and installing a Coca-Cola bottle opener for the housewives while they were there. If that wasn't enough to encourage consumption, the company also gave away—by the millions—copies of a home entertaining book written by a popular radio hostess of the day. Her suggestions included serving "Coca-Cola or tomato juice cocktails ... with canapes" and "dramatizing the breakfast occasion" with, among other treats, "grape fruit sections in Coca-Cola."

196

By 1930, Coke was spending almost $400,000 a year on radio, including sponsoring a sports show hosted by the well-known sportswriter Grantland Rice. (A Woodruff pal, Rice launched the show by interviewing Ty Cobb and another of Woodruff's friends—his golfing partner, the legendary Bobby Jones Jr.) Soon, the company would turn its attention to the booming movie industry, as well. The company's Los Angeles bottlers hired a former film producer from the silent movie era to hand out the product on back lots all across Hollywood: five cases a day for all current productions, Mark Pendergrast reports, and two cases every month for major stars. When Spencer Tracy asked for "two Coca-Colas please" in the 1939 film *Test Pilot*, Coke got all the payback it could ask for. Associating your product with a brave test pilot in those perilous times was just what the company wanted to do.

&

"It isn't what a product is but what it does that interests us," Archie Lee had written Woodruff, and the one thing Coke did was to tie itself relentlessly, and in the best possible light, to the seminal moments of American life and history.

Coke went to the Olympic games for the first time in 1928, when a thousand cases of the soft drink were sent along with the United States team to Amsterdam. It went again in 1932, to Los Angeles, and to the 1936 Olympics in Berlin. While Hitler glowered at the African-American U.S. sprinter and long jumper Jesse Owens and his four gold medals, Coca-Cola was busy inundating athletes and visitors with huge quantities of the soft drink turned out by its highly successful German bottling operation. And so the soft drink has had a major presence at every Olympics since, including the 1996 "Coca-Cola Olympic Games" in Atlanta.

When the American economy turned sour in the 1930s, Coca-Cola was there also, bearing the subliminal message that things would get better, that life was sure to turn around. Rather than paint the grim reality of the times, Coke's Depression era ads show the soft drink being consumed at Mardi Gras, the Kentucky Derby, in the shadow of the Old Faithful geyser, and at other similar oases from the grinding need and plummeting values of the time. For a mere nickel, a Coca-Cola would help you "bounce back to normal," a new Archie Lee slogan promised. By the end of 1941, "bouncing back to normal" seemed a long way to go, and Coke seized that moment, too.

In a lifetime of brilliant marketing moves, Robert Woodruff made no move more brilliant than the 25 words he uttered shortly after Japanese airplanes had destroyed the U.S. Navy base at Pearl Harbor: "We will see that every man in uniform gets a bottle of Coca-Cola for five cents, wherever he is and whatever it costs our company." Beyond doubt, patriotism underlaid the pledge, but in this case, patriotism, image enhancement, and brand building walked hand in hand.

To prove the company's dedication to the war effort, Coke sold 23,000 bags of stockpiled sugar to the U.S. military. To make sure it would have all the sugar it needed during the war, the company almost simultaneously began producing a pamphlet entitled "Importance of the Rest-Pause in Maximum War Effort." Not surprisingly, the "rest-pause" the pamphlet ultimately had in mind was the pause that refreshes: "Men work better refreshed," the "scientific study" concluded. "Time rules the present as never before. A nation at war strains forward in productive effort in a new tempo. . . . In times like these Coca-Cola is doing a necessary job for workers." Not surprisingly, either, the effort paid off. While other soft-drink makers had to make do with 80 percent of their prewar sugar supply, Coke chugged along on full sugar rations so long as the soda-pop being produced was meant for soldiers. And were the soldiers ever glad of it.

"Today was such a big day that I had to write and tell you about it," one Army private wrote home to his brother in a 1944 letter from Italy. "Everyone in the company got a Coca-Cola. That might not seem like much to you, but I wish you could see some of these guys who have been overseas for twenty months. They clutch their Coke to their chest, run to their tent and just look at it. No one has drunk theirs yet, for after you drink it, it's gone; so they don't know what to do."

Under the banner of its hit radio show "Victory Parade of Spotlight Bands," Coke sent popular groups to play at military bases all over the country. On Christmas Day, 1942, in cooperation with the Navy Department, the company sponsored a show it called "Uncle Sam's Christmas Tree": 43 orchestras performing live from 43 U.S. bases. To make sure that kids too young to fight didn't miss the message, or the chance to participate in the war effort, the company sold for a dime a youth-oriented booklet called "Know Your War Planes."

"It's the Real Thing," the company had first proclaimed in a 1942 ad. By the end of World War II, Coca-Cola was all of that. Mark Pendergrast cites an article headlined "Millions Cheer Ike at Parade Here," from the *Washington Times-Herald* of June 19, 1945:

> After feasting copiously at the Statler luncheon yesterday, Gen. Eisenhower was asked if he wished anything else.
> "Could somebody get me a Coke?" he asked.
> After polishing off the soft drink, the General said he had one more request. Asked what he wanted, he answered:
> "Another Coke."

Soon thereafter, Ike and Robert Woodruff became golfing pals.

By war's end, Coca-Cola's profits were over $100 million a year, and the soft drink had become part of the personal history of 11 million returning soldiers, sailors, and airmen. In a 1948 poll conducted by *American Legion Magazine,* nearly 64 percent of veterans named Coke as their favorite soft drink. Pepsi, which had been gaining market share before the war, was favored by fewer than 8 percent. That same year, profit on sales reached $126 million, more than 5 times Pepsi's profit. Ever the zealot, Woodruff refused to let the word "Pepsi" cross his lips.

Maybe even more important than winning the hearts and souls of American GIs, the war effort had introduced Coca-Cola to millions of soldiers and non-combatants throughout Europe and Asia—a "sampling and expansion job aboard which would have taken 25 years and millions of dollars," as one internal company document put it. Now, with the war over and the American market all but conquered, Robert Woodruff set out to subdue the rest of the world.

Almost overnight, it seemed, Woodruff had licensed 1,300 bottling plants and begun advertising in dozen of languages. Soon Coke was selling 50 million soft drinks a day, everywhere from Aruba to Australia. Eventually, under Woodruff's reign the company would set up bottling plants in 72 countries, and it would sell its products in 70 more. In 1960, it added a new container to the arsenal—a metal can that had been developed to send Coke to the troops in Korea. What worked in World War II was put to work again.

Not all the foreign invasions were easy. An earlier attempt in the mid-1920s to expand to global markets had run up against often sloppy fieldwork. The Chinese characters for "Coca-Cola," the company discovered, translated literally "bite the wax tadpole." "Refresh Yourself with Coca-Cola" came out in Dutch roughly as "Wash Your Hands with Coca-Cola." An attempt to push the drink in Cuba with skywriting took a beating when a gust of wind turned "Tome Coca-Cola" into

"Teme Coca-Cola": "Fear Coca-Cola," not "Drink Coca Cola." This second time around Coke crashed and burned in a number of cultures, less from bad advance work than from a reaction to what was seen as the ubiquity and vulgarity of American advertising.

In New York City, consumers were conditioned to electrified billboards that screamed out the virtue of products day and night. Even in rural America, radios were playing more than four hours a day, filling the air with advertising jingles and promises. In Paris and Rome, though, and in the small towns of the Old World, Coca-Cola was seen by many as the vanguard of an American commercial invasion that would wipe out domestic businesses and impose a crass New World esthetic. Outraged Italians dumped Coke in the streets of Rome, while the French complained of an attack on their national identity. One French newspaper announced that "Coca-Colonization" was a threat to Western civilization—or at least to French winemakers and their wine-loving consumers. Even the moderate *Le Monde* likened Coca-Cola's advertising to Nazi propaganda. The French government even introduced a bill that would have banned the drink, and a French political party produced a public-service short denouncing Coca-Cola. Inflamed, the people took matters into their own hands. At a Coke-sponsored French bicycle race, angry spectators threw debris on the track; elsewhere, mobs overturned company delivery trucks. But all, finally, to no avail. Robert Woodruff had a product and a mission, and as always he wasn't going to be deterred.

Coca-Cola's first international convention was held in Atlantic City in 1948, amidst an almost evangelical air. "May Providence give us the faith... to serve those two billion customers who are only waiting for us to bring our product to them," one company executive prayed. A placard on display at the convention assured attendees that "When we think of

201

Communists, we think of the Iron Curtain, BUT when THEY think of democracy, they think of Coca-Cola." Two years later, you could find Coke bottling plants in Algeria, Barbados, the Congo, Cyprus, Egypt, Gibraltar, India, Iraq, Kenya, Lebanon, Liberia, Morocco, Rhodesia, Saudi Arabia, Thailand, and Tunisia, to only scratch the surface.

"WORLD & FRIEND," the caption proclaimed on the cover of the May 15, 1950, issue of *Time* magazine. "Love that piaster, that lira, that tickey, and that American way of life." The image showed a smiling Coca-Cola disk with a skinny arm holding a Coke bottle up for a thirsty globe to drink from. *Time* made it official: Robert Woodruff had won. Coke was not just an American drink anymore; it was, as the journalist William Allen White had once described it, "the sublimated essence of all that America stands for." And *Time* had good reason to celebrate the victory: Woodruff was a hunting pal of *Time* co-founder Henry Luce.

"My job is to sell Coca-Cola, to see that as many people as possible are able to enjoy it," Woodruff had once said. "I am not a seer, an oracle, or a philosopher, and I doubt that my opinions on an endless variety of public issues would be sufficiently informed or authoritative to make them either useful or interesting." It was by dint of such single-mindedness that he managed to turn sugared water into a billion dollar corporation.

⁂

Robert Woodruff was 95 years old and near death on January 1, 1985, when Roberto Goizueta came to pay a call. The Cuban-born Goizueta was by then CEO of Coca-Cola, a post Woodruff had given up years earlier, but in the corporate culture of Coke, Woodruff still loomed monstrous, and Goizueta had come for his blessing. Blind taste test after blind taste test showed that soft-drink consumers preferred Pepsi to Coke,

Goizueta informed the Boss. In time, no matter how much you spent on advertising and how good the ads were, those numbers would catch up with you. It was time to change the formula. Goizueta wanted Woodruff's blessing for a product that was to be known as New Coke—a clear winner over Pepsi and old Coke in the same blind taste tests.

"Do it," Woodruff is said to have finally rasped, his eyes heavy with tears.

Early that spring, New Coke hit the market and quickly proved one of the most spectacular product failures of the century. Robert Woodruff, though, wasn't around to witness the wreck. Soon after giving his blessing to the reformulated soft drink, Woodruff stopped eating, Mark Pendergrast recounts. By the time New Coke flamed out, the Boss was in his grave a month. So well, though, had Coca-Cola learned the lessons that Robert Woodruff taught it that even the debacle of New Coke didn't matter much in the long run: Three years after the New Coke debacle, an independent survey found that old Coke was the best known, most admired trademark in the world.

11

TIME WARNER
Turning Opposing Cultures to Common Advantage

N THE FALL OF 1989, TOP OFFICIALS OF TIME INC., the most recognizable name in the world of print journalism, and Warner Communications, the world's largest entertainment company, gathered in the Caribbean to celebrate their pending union. Only three years earlier, General Electric had purchased RCA, the parent company of National Broadcasting Company, for $6.4 billion, in what was then the largest non-oil acquisition in U.S. history. A few months earlier, Capital Cities picked up American Broadcasting Company for $3.5 billion. In November 1989 Sony paid $3.4 billion for Columbia Pictures Entertainment. In the communications and entertainment industry, everything that rises was converging. Now the biggest of the big had done just that: When it was completed in January 1990, the Time Warner merger would create the largest media conglomerate the world had ever known, worth $14.1 billion.

Time Inc. brought to the marriage nearly seventy years of publishing experience, beginning with the flagship newsweekly founded in 1922 by Henry Luce and Briton Hadden with $86,000 borrowed from Luce's friends. In the 1930s Luce added *Fortune* and *Life* to *Time*—the man had a genius for magazine titles. *Sports Illustrated* came along in the 1950s, another category killer. By the late 1980s, though, Henry Luce had been dead for two decades, and the printed word and image no longer ruled the empire he had launched. Luce had resisted television, even turning down a chance in the early days of the industry to buy one of the networks, but within two years of his death, Time was beginning to remake itself into a communications giant, not just a print one. The HBO movie channel and Time's extensive TV cable-system holdings were what caught Warner Communications' eye.

For its part, Warner Communications had traveled both a more direct and a more tortured path to the corporate altar. Motion pictures in anything like a modern form had been born in 1894 when Thomas Edison perfected his Kinetoscope, and the four Warner brothers had been there almost from the beginning. Jack Warner, the youngest, wasn't yet in his teens when the brothers set up a tent in their backyard to show their first movie. By the 1920s, Jack Warner had made it to Hollywood as a film producer and even had a star under contract: Rin-Tin-Tin. The famous German Shepherd, Warner would later say, was the most reliable employee in the studio's history—never asked for a raise, never demanded a close up. In 1927, over older-brother Harry's objection, the Warners put up $4 million so that audiences could hear Al Jolson say "Wait a minute . . . wait a minute. You ain't heard nothin' yet!" in *The Jazz Singer*, and with that, the Warners' fortune was made and the history of motion pictures changed forever. In that final year of the silent era, motion picture receipts reached $769 million. Two years later, in 1929, with the studios tripping all over themselves to turn out the new talkies, receipts had grown 19 percent, to $913 million.

The Warner brothers would eventually fall out bitterly, and the studio they founded would pass through a variety of hands, some of them passing strange. Seven Arts Ltd. was the first to purchase Warner Bros., in 1967, by which time it was producing more television series than any other major studio. Two years later, Seven Arts turned around and sold Warner to Kinney National Services, publishers of the *Superman* comics and the irrepressible *Mad* magazine. Three years later Kinney changed the name to Warner Communications, and Warner became not just a movie and TV company, but an entertainment one, with everything from sitcoms to amusement parks huddled under the corporate umbrella. But it wasn't the rollercoaster rides that brought Time knocking on Warner Bros.'s door. It was the TV serials Warner had retained the rights to and the movies in its vault—classics like *Little Caesar, Casablanca,* and *Rebel Without a Cause.*

Warner had content, in short. Time had conduit. In the new calculus of the communication–entertainment industry, such synergy was irresistible. And never mind that the companies had cultures, corporate histories, and founders as different as newsprint and celluloid.

⌘

A Polish peasant who emigrated to Baltimore in 1883, Benjamin Warner and his wife, Pearl Leah Eichelbaum, would have nine children, but it was the four brothers—Harry, Abe, Jack, and Sam—who put the family name (which Benjamin adopted in 1907) in spotlights. A cobbler in Poland, Benjamin opened a shoe repair shop when he got to the New World; moved on to selling notions from a wagon, dragging his family through a succession of addresses across the East and into Canada; and eventually settled in Youngstown, Ohio, where he kept kosher, lived within walking distance of a synagogue, and commonly conversed in Yiddish. The older brothers, Harry and Abe, would inherit their father's devoutness. More assimilated, the younger two, and particularly Jack, would resist it.

Jack, who left school after the fourth grade, once explained that he had paid little attention to the rabbi his father hired to tutor the children in religion: "I didn't dig it at all." An eyewitness remembered another occasion when Harry was showing a visiting rabbi around the house: "Harry introduced the rabbi to Jack, and Jack said, 'How're ya, rab? I caught your act at the Palace. You were great!'" Both remarks are typical of the brother who would come—by hook *and* by crook—to rule the family business.

It was Sam Warner who really got the brothers into film. After he bought a film projector from an acquaintance in 1903, using his siblings' pooled savings, the brothers set up a tent in their Youngstown backyard and began charging admission to see the movie that had come with the projector—*The Great Train Robbery*. Before long, Sam and Abe were taking the projector on the road, showing *The Great Train Robbery* at a succession of small towns and wherever crowds were likely to gather. One early stop in Niles, Ohio—in a rented store near a carnival encampment—netted the brothers $300 in a single week. In 1906, weary of the road, the four Warners set up shop in New Castle, Pennsylvania, a steel town about fifteen miles across the state line from Youngstown. The Cascade, as they fancied their theater, used seats borrowed from a neighboring funeral parlor. Harry rented the films and Abe kept the books, while Sam ran the projector and a sister, Rose, played the piano. Jack, who was later to perform at the Youngstown Opera House under the exotic name of Leon Zuardo and as a boy soprano with a vaudeville troupe, sang between movie showings, mostly to chase people out of the theater.

The Cascade proved a success, but so long as they were simply renting and showing other people's films in a single location, the brothers calculated that theirs would never be more than success with a small "s." In 1907, just as Jack was turning 15, the Warners moved to Pittsburgh and created the

Duquesne Film Exchange, with the purpose of buying films and renting them out to other distributors. It was a first tentative step at taking themselves national.

Commercially, Duquesne took off. Soon, the business was operating not just in Pennsylvania and Ohio, but in Virginia, Maryland, and Georgia as well. Legally, though, there were problems. Through the Motion Pictures Patents Company, Thomas Edison controlled all film patents and the right to collect licensing fees from anyone who sought to make movies or show them commercially. Like others in the growing movie business, the Warners fought the obligation, and the Justice Department smashed it for good with a 1912 antitrust suit, a year after the Supreme Court had ordered John D. Rockefeller's Standard Oil broken up. By then, the Duquesne film business had been sold off, and Harry had sent Sam and Jack to St. Louis to begin producing cheap two-reel films.

The results—movies such as *The Perils of the Plains*—are by common consent painful to watch, so painful indeed that the brothers were soon back in the distribution business, this time with Harry and Abe moving to New York, where they would continue to pay attention to the books and other business matters, while Jack and Sam set up shop in Los Angeles, near Hollywood where the film industry was beginning to consolidate. Among other advantages, producers could shoot films year-round in southern California's temperate climate.

The Warners continued to dabble in filmmaking—they were never content to be down the movie food-chain—and in 1917, more than a dozen years after they had first begun to nibble at the corners of the industry, the brothers finally had their first commercial hit. *My Four Years in Germany* had been a bestselling book by the former U.S. ambassador to Berlin, James W. Gerard. In the Warners' hands, the book became a supremely jingoistic movie filled with heartless Huns, violated women, and tortured innocents. For World War I America, it was just the right combination. The movie opened in December 1917, six months after the first U.S. troops had arrived in Europe. By the time it was through its run, the Warners had netted $130,000 on $1.5 million in gross receipts, a handsome enough profit to allow Jack and Sam to set up their own small studio on Hollywood's Poverty Row. The war was also to bring Jack Warner his sole shot at fame on the other side of the camera: As a member of the Army Signal Corps, he got to star in a training film about the dangers of sexually transmitted diseases.

By 1923, the Warners had incorporated themselves as Warner Bros. Pictures, Inc. Two years later they picked up Vitagraph, a failing filmmaker but one with a national distribution chain in place. With the further addition of major-market theaters, the brothers had achieved the fundamental structure of a major studio without the track record of one. Warner Bros. movies still were made on the cheap, often as knockoffs of popular movies and popular actors. Lacking the resources to hire Charlie Chaplin, for example, the brothers hired his brother, Sydney. Neither the audiences nor the other studios were much fooled.

Thanks especially to Sam Warner, though, all that was about to change. Jack and Sam were both present in 1925 when a sound engineer told them that Bell Labs was developing a technique that would allow movie makers to synchronize sound and film. For the established studios like MGM and Paramount, the new technology held little allure: They were doing just fine without introducing sound into their very profitable world of silent films. The upstart studios, though, had less invested in the status quo and far less to lose by taking the plunge.

Years later, Harry Warner would recall the meeting that changed the course of movie history. Harry had thought he was attending a gathering of Wall Street bankers; instead, it was a demonstration of sound movies. "I am positive if [Sam had] said 'talking pictures,' I would not have gone," Harry said. The process, he had thought, was "foolish bunk." With the demonstration, though, even the most cautious of the brothers was sold. With Sam at the lead—and just in front of their equally ambitious movie competitor William Fox—the Warner brothers signed a contract with Bell Labs to produce a series of shorts using a sound process the Bell people had dubbed Vitaphone, and committed the first of what would eventually add up to $4 million in movie development costs. And with that the movies would be silent no more.

The first demonstration of the Vitaphone process came on August 6, 1926, before a packed Warner Theater on Broadway. Apart from historical reasons, the program wasn't particularly memorable: a series of shorts prepared by Sam Warner at the old Vitagraph studios in Brooklyn, followed by *Don Juan,* a full-length film made by Jack in Hollywood, featuring what the Warner Bros. rarely had, a legitimate star in John Barrymore. Nor for that matter was the technology all that riveting: The Vitaphone process played only a musical soundtrack that underscored the action, not the dialogue itself. But even such relatively simple technology had a riveting effect.

"The morning after the successful premiere of *Don Juan,* *Variety* issued a special edition in acknowledgement of the impending revolution," the film historian Neal Gabler has written. "Warner Bros. stock soared from $8 to $65 per share. The Warners became very wealthy men overnight."

The success was short lived. The Vitaphone equipment—essentially a huge record player synchronized with a projector—was so expensive to install and so difficult to operate that, despite the success of *Don Juan,* many theaters refused to order it. Nor were the subsequent Vitaphone movies, including another forgettable comedy with the substitute Chaplin, Sydney, up to the standards of the first, either in quality or in surprise value. By the end of 1926, the Warner Bros. studio was $1 million in the red for the year, better than the previous year but hardly an omen of success. The brothers, however, had seen the future, and they had no intention of being denied their place in it.

For $50,000 the studio secured the rights to a Broadway play about an aged cantor and his runaway son who, rather than follow in his father's tradition, is drawn to singing in night-clubs. When the father falls sick on Yom Kippur, the Jewish day of atonement, his congregation urges the estranged son to take the old cantor's place singing the Kol Nidre, the traditional plea for forgiveness, and therein lies the great dilemma: Yom Kip-pur also happens to be the day the son's long-sought big chance, his own Broadway revue, is to open. On the stage, the part of the son had been played to critical and popular success by George Jessel: The play enjoyed a 38-week Broadway run. Although the Warners presumably had seen their movie as a Jessel vehicle, too, Jack and Sam soon decided to replace him with one of the most popular singers of the day, Al Jolson. They did keep the play's name, however—*The Jazz Singer.*

The year 1927 was rife with historic events: Babe Ruth's sixtieth home run, Charles Lindbergh's solo flight across the Atlantic in *The Spirit of St. Louis,* and the execution of two immigrant anarchists named Nicola Sacco and Bartolomeo Vanzetti were only some of the most notable. But few moments in that memorable year, and no other moment in cinema his-tory, was equal in impact to the opening of *The Jazz Singer* on October 6. By the time Jolson had closed the movie singing his trademark black-face number "Mammy," it was obvious to everyone in attendance that a night at the movies would never be the same again.

Neal Gabler wrote:

> The evening was brisk and clear, and the theater on Broadway was filled with notables. If they were waiting for an answer to the

question of sound, they soon got it. One young Paramount executive raced into the lobby during intermission and called his boss in California: "This is a revolution." When the movie's star, Al Jolson, strode to the stage to be showered by the audience's plaudits, tears rolled down his cheeks. The next morning Adolph Zukor called about 50 Paramount executives to the Savoy-Plaza suite and demanded to know why they hadn't made a sound film. The same scene was being re-enacted throughout the industry.

Among the few important movie people in New York to miss the opening night were four of the most newly important of them all: the Warner brothers. In a scene that it would seem only Hollywood could write, Sam Warner, who had been more responsible than anyone in the studio and maybe anyone in the industry for pushing sound, died of a heart attack 24 hours before *The Jazz Singer* made its first public appearance.

With the release of The Jazz Singer, Warner Bros. stock, which had sunk back down to $9 a share, skyrocketed to $132, and Harry, always the business mastermind of the studio, moved to consolidate the success and grow the holdings. By the end of the decade, Warner Bros. was adding one new theater a day to its stable, purchasing record companies, radio stations, and foreign patents, and backing Broadway shows. Rin-Tin-Tin, found by a patrol of U.S. airmen in an abandoned German war-dog station during World War I, gave the Warners a proven moneymaker at the box office. With the acquisition of First National Pictures in 1930, they added a Burbank studio, an improved film-distribution chain, and a line-up of non-canine stars that included Basil Rathbone and Loretta Young.

Led by Jack Warner in Hollywood, the studio was also developing a formula for a new kind of gritty, inexpensive movie—one ripped from the day's headlines, shot on city streets with actors the public could identify with, playing people like themselves: truck drivers and boxers, journalists and working men. In movies like the 1930 *Little Caesar* and *The Public Enemy* (1931), the studio caught the spirit of the new hard times. Through Busby Berkeley's lush musical extravaganzas, it also kept a strong presence in the escapist movies typical of the decade. And with movies like *Disraeli* (1930), the anti-lynching *They Won't Forget* (1937), and the 1939 *Confessions of a Nazi Spy*, the first significant American antifascist film, the studio also showed a social conscience. Thanks to both Jack and Harry Warner, in their different ways, and to a growing stable of box-office winners that now included James Cagney, Edward G. Robinson, Humphrey Bogart, and Bette Davis, Warner Bros. weathered the Depression as well as any studio.

By the late 1930s, the surviving Warner brothers were legitimate Hollywood moguls, heads of a studio that was earning almost $180 million a year, but with Sam's death and the death of their parents within a few months of each other eight years later, the fragile truce that had existed between Harry and Jack began to break down completely. Great movies would still come out of Warner Bros.—*Casablanca*, for example, in 1942, and *Watch on the Rhine* the next year—but the studio system that had helped the Warners and other early movie moguls amass their fortunes wasn't long for this world. In 1948, the government decreed that the studios had to sell off their theater chains. With that, a system as vertically integrated as any Henry Ford had dreamed of came to an end. More and more, too, the most titillating stories out of Warner Bros. were about the brothers themselves.

In 1915, shortly after moving to Los Angeles, Jack had married Irma Solomon and almost immediately begun chasing young women all around town and developing a well-earned reputation for infidelity. Jack's passions finally settled on a lovely bit-actress named Ann Page Alvarado, with whom he began living openly before either of their divorces was final. In 1935, only two months after his father's death, Jack and Ann were married. For the devout and moralistic Harry, who could accept neither the unfaithfulness nor Ann's Catholicism, it was one more blow in a stormy relationship: He regularly referred to Ann around the studio as Jack's "whore," and he and his own wife for the most part refused to see her. Worse was yet to come.

In 1956, more than three decades after the brothers had formed their studio and a year after scoring a major hit with the James Dean vehicle *Rebel Without a Cause*, the three surviving Warners agreed to sell the studio—or so Harry and Abe thought. On the side, Jack made a deal to buy back his own stock and stay on as head of the studio, now without his brothers. Even before the news of the double-dealing reached Harry, he had refused to enter the studio commissary if Jack was anywhere around. Informed of Jack's treachery, Harry took a lead pipe and, despite his 75 years, began chasing his brother all over the lot, shouting that he was going to kill him and failing, perhaps, only when his last desperate effort to throw the pipe at Jack went wide.

The next year, when Harry and his wife were celebrating their fiftieth wedding anniversary, Jack showed up unexpected, commandeered a glass of champagne, and demanded: "Where's Harry? I'm busting my balls at the studio and he's living the good life." When Harry died in 1958, his widow Rea was quoted as saying: "Harry didn't die. Jack killed him." In any event, Jack didn't attend the funeral: He was vacationing on the Riviera with Darryl Zanuck at the time. Nor did he manage to mention Harry in his autobiography, *My First Hundred Years in Hollywood*.

In 1964 after yet another family blowup, Jack Warner locked his own son and namesake, Jack Jr., out of the studio and barely spoke to him again. Two years later, in 1966, he sold Warner Bros. again, this time for good. When he died another dozen years later in Los Angeles, Jack Warner had a nearly unequaled reputation in the industry for boorishness and bad manners. He also could lay claim, along with his brothers, to having taken part in the production of some five thousand movies and to being in on the birth of some of the most revolutionary entertainment innovations of the twentieth century. For good and sometimes for their own ill, Jack, Harry, Sam, and Abe Warner had ridden the movie boom straight to the top.

⋙

If Jack Warner had a polar opposite in his lifetime—a secret good twin to his evil one—it would seem to be Henry Luce. Born in Tengchow, China, in 1898 to missionary parents, Luce would help to elect presidents and set American foreign policy for decades on either side of World War II. The poet Carl Sandburg once called him the "greatest journalist of all time." More sweepingly and probably more accurately, University of Chicago president Robert M. Hutchins, perhaps the most influential educator of his day, would contend that Luce, through his magazines, did more to shape the American character than "the whole education system put together." However you cut it, here was a man who mattered.

Luce's father, a Presbyterian minister, ran a small college in Tengchow (now P'eng-lai), where Chinese converts to Christianity could receive instruction. Except for very occasional visits to relatives in the United States, "Harry" Luce would spend his entire childhood in China, and he would never forget the lessons he learned at the college and in the walled compound where he lived with his father and mother, a one-time social worker for the Young Women's Christian Association. For the entirety of his life, even when he had become one of the most powerful publishing magnates in the world, Luce would pray on his knees before going to bed. (Religion, he once explained, was a "goddamn good thing.") Nor would Luce forget the global view he learned at the knee of his father and the other missionaries working to convert and educate the heathen: America was superior to other nations, just as Christianity was superior to other religions, and capitalism was superior to all other economic systems. What's more, as a superior nation and people, America and Americans had both the obligation and the divine duty to lead the world out of darkness. Not surprisingly, Theodore Roosevelt was his lifelong hero.

Intelligent, determined, and endowed with a moral certainty he would never lose, Luce set off from China in 1913, at age 15, on a solo, four-month journey through Europe that eventually ended him up at the Hotchkiss School in Wallingford, Connecticut, one of the traditional bastions of the elite and what was then considered an enlightened blue-blood education. Three years later he would enroll in another all-white, all-male, nearly all-Protestant institution, Yale College, where he would join that ultimate redoubt of the Establishment, Skull & Bones, later home to, among others, two George Bushes. A scholarship student who helped pay his tuition at both schools through a succession of menial jobs, Luce nonetheless shared a sense of noblesse oblige with his more wealthy and connected classmates: a feeling that they were destined to lead. For Henry Luce, journalism would become the avenue toward the fulfillment of that destiny.

Trained on the Hotchkiss school newspaper, Luce helped to edit the *Yale Daily News*, where he so impressed his classmates that he was voted the "most brilliant" member of the Class of 1920. After a postgraduate stint at Oxford University, he returned to the states and worked on newspapers in Chicago and Baltimore. For a Yale graduate, newspaper work was almost indecent in the 1920s—A.J. Liebling once called newspapers "a refuge for the vaguely talented"—but daily journalism was only a way station in Henry Luce's plans.

Ever since 1918, he and his Hotchkiss and Yale friend Brit Hadden had been talking about creating a new form of journalism that wouldn't just report events but would interpret them and do so with what in modern terms might be called an "attitude"—a kind of irreverent cleverness. Like Jack Warner, Luce and Hadden both wanted to entertain readers. Entertainment had suddenly become not just a diversion in a more leisure-oriented society; it had also become big business. But ever the missionary's son, Luce also intended to instruct readers in his own world view.

In 1923, Luce and Hadden borrowed $86,000 from some of their well-connected school friends and created the world's first newsweekly. They called it *Time*—"the most precious commodity we have," Luce was to say—and true to the name and its intent, pieces were edited so that the whole product could be read cover to cover in less than an hour. To grab the reader's attention, the two founders created a breezy style for the magazine and a unique diction. Hadden, especially, had an ear for then-rare usages that *Time* turned into commonplaces—words such as "tycoon," "socialite," and "kudos." For material, the editors culled stories from newspapers around the country, often compelling human-interest tales that made an easy connection with the educated, mostly middle-class audience Luce was aiming for. To speed their digestion, the stories were compressed into what one critic dismissed as "the capsulized abridgement of a condensation." A fast read, though, was not meant to be an empty one: Luce always saw his magazine as feeding "true" Americans hungry for knowledge, and feeding them a very specific diet that also happened to be entirely aligned with Henry Luce's own moderate conservatism. *Time* favored civil rights and opposed the Ku Klux Klan—it enraged segregationists by documenting lynchings, and Luce himself was a major supporter of both the Urban League and the United Negro College Fund. *Time* also was for evolution and against fundamentalism. It disliked Communism with a vengeance, was dismissive of Prohibition, and thought atheists were (at best) off their rockers. And sometimes to make sure that no one missed the message or got it wrong, Luce and his editors were not above ignoring inconvenient facts.

Intellectuals, for the most part, hated the magazine, but intellectuals are, after all, few in number. The middle class felt differently, and that's what counted. In 1927, *Time* turned its first small profit. Two years later, Henry Luce and Brit Hadden were millionaires. Hadden wouldn't get to enjoy the ride—he died suddenly in 1929 of a blood infection—but for Luce and Time Inc. the good times were just beginning.

In 1930, convinced that businessmen needed help in under-standing a rapidly changing society, Luce launched a business magazine that he called *Fortune*. As if to reinforce the point, he charged a small fortune to buy it: $1 an issue, equivalent to nearly $9.50 in today's dollars. Perhaps the formula shouldn't have worked—the nation's economic strength was nearing its nadir—but it did. Luce hired talent to staff the magazine, he paid well, insisted the publication be well researched and printed on the best paper with top photography, and he gave the talent he brought on board the freedom to follow their instincts. Within a few years, *Fortune* was publishing a ground-breaking journalistic study of anti-Semitism in American busi-ness. *Let Us Now Praise Famous Men*. James Agee and Walker Evans's passionate and lyrical look at white poverty in rural Alabama, never appeared in *Fortune's* pages, but the book began as a *Fortune* assignment.

Suddenly an important figure on Wall Street now that his reporters were covering it, Luce charged ahead, buying *Archi-tectural Forum* magazine and launching "The March of Time," a series of documentary films that soon were being shown in movie theaters around the world. Convinced that he could make a large-scale pictorial magazine succeed where many others had failed, Luce in the mid-1930s bought the rights to a defunct publication with the catchy title of *Life*. By late 1936, he was ready to launch his own version under the same name.

Like *Time* and *Fortune*, *Life* magazine would not only reflect the world as it was, this time in pictures; it would also crusade for a better planet, one without injustice and inequality. But *Life* was also a way for Luce to show readers all sorts of things about the world that wouldn't fall under the normal category of news. He himself had an insatiable curiosity, and he assumed his readers would share it. Luce wanted people, he once said, "to see *Life*—to see, and be amazed." And amazed, indeed, they were. All 466,000 copies of the first issue sold out on the very first day the magazine went on sale. Before long, one in every three Americans was reading *Life* every week, and *Life* had become—and still remains—the most popular magazine in American history. By the end of World War II, Henry Luce stood astride one of the largest and wealthiest publishing enterprises the world had ever known.

⌁

As was the case with the Warner brothers, Henry Luce's life would prove that great financial success does not necessarily translate into great happiness or domestic bliss. Like Jack Warner, Luce shed a wife as he grew famous and married a beauty in her place: Clare Boothe Brokaw, an editor, playwright, later a member of the House of Representatives, and an ambassador. Like Jack Warner, Henry Luce also quickly developed a taste for the high life as his fortune grew and grew. Never the happiest of married couples, Henry and Clare Boothe Luce lived in mansions, spent lavishly on art, and stayed in the best hotel suites wherever they went.

Unlike Jack Warner, though, there was never anything trivial about Henry Luce's aspirations. When he wasn't making films, Warner passed his time gambling, playing tennis, and before he met and married Ann, chasing women. Luce, in the words of former *Time* editor-in-chief Henry Grunwald, "saw himself as God's collaborator. He felt he was doing God's work." For Luce, that meant using his money and position to become involved in the great issues of his time.

"On the issues and people he cared most about—China, American foreign policy, the Republican Party, Chiang Kai-shek, Winston Churchill, Wendell Wilkie—he personally directed coverage at critical times with a feverish and occasional suffocating intensity. And on those subjects his magazines could be startlingly biased, even polemical," the historian Alan Brinkley wrote in Luce's first magazine, on the centenary of his birth.

Luce had little use for Franklin Roosevelt or his New Deal, but he backed the president wholeheartedly in the years leading up to World War II, when Roosevelt appeared to be leaning toward helping the Allied powers and rearming the United States, and he threw the entire editorial weight of his publishing empire behind the Lend-Lease Bill's proposal to ship aging U.S. naval vessels to Great Britain. In the winter of 1941, in what was to become a famous essay, Luce argued in *Life* magazine that America had both the duty and the opportunity to determine the outcome of the coming global conflagration and to lead the world toward freedom and order in the aftermath of an Allied victory. He called the article "The American Century," one more proof of his genius for compact phrasing.

Whatever promise Luce had found in FDR had withered by 1940. Not only did Luce play a key role in gaining the Republican presidential nomination for Wendell Wilkie; he tried to protect his investment by having the managing editor of *Fortune* run the Wilkie campaign and write most of his important speeches. When Wilkie backed away from the internationalism Luce favored and began courting isolationists like Charles Lindbergh, Luce complained that he should have "told the truth and gone down, with greater honor, in a far greater defeat." Twelve years later, he picked a better horse to ride and throw his media empire behind: Dwight D. Eisenhower. And by the mid-1950s Luce had power to burn. *Time* was selling two million issues a week; *Life* was selling six million; and the newly launched *Sports Illustrated* was looking like a winner as well. By 1955, Time Inc. was bringing in annual revenues of over $200 million, and Henry Luce had a wonderful new place to stay whenever he visited Rome. Ike had expressed his thanks to the publisher by making Clare Boothe Luce ambassador to Italy.

Internationally, Luce was always true to his formative years in China. He abhorred Communism, fought the diplomatic recognition of Mao Zedong's China, pushed wherever and however he could for military and economic aid to the Nationalist Chinese government on Taiwan, and lent both his name and money to a fistful of groups with names like the Committee to Aid Refugee Chinese Intellectuals. Luce fought the spread of Communism into Korea as well and, later, into South Vietnam. Even after he stepped down from the chairmanship in 1964, *Time* continued to be a strident (and finally almost a lonely) supporter of the American war effort there.

In retirement, Alan Brinkley writes in his *Time* centenary tribute, Luce continued to be the missionary's son, still seeking spiritual and emotional fulfillment—"a search so intense that he and Clare reportedly experimented occasionally with LSD, on the advice of friends who described it as a vehicle of awakening."

⌘

Henry Luce and Jack Warner would be long in their graves by the time the two empires they founded completed their merger in January 1990: Luce died suddenly of a heart attack at age 68 in 1967, 11 years before Warner was carried off by a stroke. But as different as the two men and their two empires were, both seem in retrospect to have been on a collision course from the beginning. The two companies had been incorporated within months of each other. Both had resisted television only to be overwhelmed by its popularity. To Warner, television was "a bastard industry." A TV set, he vowed, would never appear in any Warner Bros. film. But that was before more than two-thirds of all Americans were watching their TV sets on a regular basis. Now, the print company had become a very profitable TV cable enterprise, and the movie studio had moved into television, theme parks, retail stores, even sports teams. Separately, though, both were having trouble competing with other media giants. Survival in the new math of the entertainment industry meant appropriating as many things as you possibly could, both cornering markets and going in every direction at once. Together, that's just what Time Warner could do, and so it was that a company formed by the son of a Christian missionary was joined to a show business outfit begun by four feisty Jewish brothers. In the synergy-driven economics of the 1990s, it didn't even seem strange.

The same set of circumstances applied in 1996 when Time Warner entered into a $7.6-billion merger with Ted Turner's Turner Broadcasting System. Turner had content and conduit, and a huge presence on cable TV that ran the gamut from Henry Luce's news reporting to the Warner brothers' movie showing and making. (What the hawkish Luce might have made of having Time Inc.'s name linked with Turner's then-wife, "Hanoi Jane" Fonda, is, of course, another matter.) Nor were the circumstances any different really when Time Warner rocked Wall Street in 1999 by announcing its pending marriage to Steve Case's Internet giant America Online. It was still a matter of content and conduit—Time Warner's and AOL's—but by century's end both had gone digital.

12

BILL GATES *and* CYBERSPACE

The Dematerialized Future

OR CENTURIES, THE CENTER OF GLOBAL ECONOMIC power has moved steadily westward from the city-states of Renaissance Italy through Spain and the Netherlands—the one grown rich on gold and silver, the other through trading in spices and stocks—to the inventors and capitalists who fueled the Industrial Revolution in England. By the mid-1800s, the locus of wealth had begun to leap the ocean to the United States, where railroads waited to be built and vast natural resources turned into individual fortunes such as the world had never known. As the American market burgeoned, so did the American demand for durable goods, and no durable good was more fitted to the American ethic than the private automobile. Advertising exploited the multiplicity of choice and helped create brands such as Coca-Cola that ruled their market, and as the world shrunk, the world became the market. The intersection of mass communication with the rise of leisure time and a leisure class turned the movie screen and the television into pots of gold for those who controlled the studios and the means of transmission. And then along came the computer and the Internet, and everything exploded yet again.

With the computer and an Internet navigation system, every home could be not just an entertainment center but a learning center, a trading center, and a communication hub, to boot. While profitable brick-and-mortar companies shrank in market value, often profitless dot.com companies soared to price/earnings ratios that could make the Dutch tulipmania of the seventeenth century seem almost sane, and yet the market roared on and on, a bull on a record run. The old rules seemed to have been broken. Wealth had dematerialized. Physical content meant almost nothing. Intellectual content meant almost everything. Information, it seemed, was everywhere. And the great trailing fortune that embodied the Information Age belonged to an $80-billion Seattle nerd named William Henry Gates III.

Like Henry Ford with his Model T, Bill Gates envisioned the mass appeal of the personal computer, but unlike Ford, he didn't want to build it. Gates's genius was never in hardware; instead, he provided the brains—the software and operating systems—that made the hardware hum. Like J.P. Morgan, Gates also saw himself as creating order out of disarray. MS-DOS and Windows weren't just operating systems and software products; they were meant to be industry standards because a standardized industry would benefit everyone—Bill Gates most particularly. Gates understood brand, too: The various iterations of his Windows software, all named by year, were introduced at press conferences that wrapped high-tech in the glitz of a Miss Universe pageant. Be there or be square, the press conferences seemed to be saying, but there was a subliminal message as well: Don't get in my way. Gates, in fact, had the ruthlessness of a John D. Rockefeller when it came to cutting down and co-opting his competition, and just as the government had broken up Rockefeller's Standard Oil, so it sought to dismantle Gates's Microsoft Corporation.

One more way that Gates resembles so many of the moguls who came before him: He began the business that was to make him the world's richest man out of nothing more than a dominating idea borne on an iron will. Henry Ford empowered his workers—and kept the unions at bay—by creating the $5 a day wage. Bill Gates empowered his workers—and kept them from fleeing to other software companies—by sharing the wealth through stock options. He wasn't the first to try the strategy, but no one had ever shared the wealth quite like this. Before the century was out, Microsoft would create more than twenty thousand in-house millionaires, from code writers to secretaries. Gates and all the others who helped launch the Information Age also shared the wealth in one more critical way that would remake the world as surely as the Industrial Revolution had done: They provided the infrastructure that anyone, anywhere on earth could use. Nearly a thousand years earlier, Godric had had to battle improbable odds simply to win the chance to raise himself out of abject poverty. Now, for the first time in human history, opportunity was universal.

⌘

Moguls, magnates, the people who create and master industries, the ones who integrate them and bring them to their fullest fruition—such business meta-successes are always many different things to many different people. To some they are saints, promises that democratic capitalism nurtures a meritocracy of the naturally talented. Others laud the John D. Rockefellers for their generosity, even as they decry the ruthlessness that propels them to the top. To still others, moguls are evil incarnate, representatives of all that's wrong in a system that not only allows but sometimes seem to thrive on the economic disparity between top and bottom. Some of the biggest of the moguls have been all things at once: Henry Ford the first billionaire, Henry Ford the social innovator, Henry Ford the almost-president, Henry Ford the creator of the modern industrial order, Henry Ford the Fascist sympathizer and rabid anti-unionist. The list of contradictions goes on and on. And so it is with Bill Gates.

No human has ever been so rich. Because Bill Gates is so heavily invested in his own company, his wealth at any given moment is tied intimately to the share price of Microsoft stock. That meant that in 1996, when the company's stock soared by 88 percent, Gates made nearly $11 billion on paper, or about $30 million a day. John D. Rockefeller was said to have earned roughly $2 a second at his prime: At his company's prime, Gates was earning at a pace nearly 175 times that—roughly $347 a second, or enough every minute to buy a new Honda Accord. True to Gates's decree that Microsoft should always have enough cash in the bank to operate for a year without any revenues, his company at the time was carrying a balance of $8 billion. With his own money, Gates built a 40,000 square foot home sunk into a bluff overlooking Lake Washington, outside Seattle. The vaulted garage alone can hold 30 cars. Modern in the extreme, this house is also palatial in the extreme—an El Escorial for the Information Age.

Rarely, too, has one human been quite so many conflicting things to quite so many people. Friends and colleagues like to talk—in the language of the digerati—about Gates's ability to "parallel process," his "unlimited bandwidth" and facility at "multitasking." They note that he works on two computers at once in his office at the sprawling Microsoft campus in Redmond, Washington: One computer sequences data coming in from the Internet, while the other handles the hundreds of daily e-mail messages through which Gates keeps in touch with his own employees and the larger world. His mind, they say, has many of the problem-solving capacities of the best computers: a knack for turning enormous input into finely crafted answers. At least in part, Gates goes along with the idea.

Gates told Walter Isaacson of *Time* magazine:

I don't think there's anything unique about human intelligence. All the neurons in the brain that make up perceptions and emotions operate in a binary fashion. We can someday replicate that on a machine. Eventually we'll be able to sequence the human genome and replicate how nature did intelligence in a carbon-based system.... It's like reverse-engineering someone else's product in order to solve a challenge.

Even Gates's famously contentious style is a positive, according to Microsoft executive Steve Ballmer, a former Harvard classmate (he graduated, Gates didn't) whom Gates lured to the company in 1980 from Procter & Gamble:

Conflict can be a good thing. The difference from P & G is striking. Politeness was at a premium there. Bill knows it's important to avoid that gentle civility that keeps you from getting to the heart of an issue quickly. He likes it when anyone, even a junior employee, challenges him, and you know he respects you when he starts shouting back.

As for Gates's softer, less binary side, supporters point to his philanthropy and to his friendship with the very low-tech billionaire, Warren Buffett, whom Gates superseded as America's richest citizen. Like Andrew Carnegie, Gates has expressed a desire to spend much of the second half of his life giving away his money, a process already underway. Through a foundation run by Gates's father, Gates and his wife, Melinda, have donated billions of dollars, mostly for education, libraries, and public health. For the year 1999, grants from the Bill & Melinda Gates Foundation included nearly $950 million for vaccines against preventable diseases and an even $1 billion to fund the Gates Millennium Scholars program, to enhance minority access to higher education. Among the points of attraction between Gates and Buffett, who is 25 years his senior, is a fascination with games of all sorts, and a marathon-like capacity to pursue them. The first time America's two richest men got together with their wives at Buffett's San Francisco home, they ended up playing nine straight hours of bridge.

Where Bill Gates is concerned, though, such benign assessments never want for counterbalance. Gates and Microsoft spent most of the 1990s under almost constant legal assault: The antitrust suit filed by the Justice Department that led to Judge Thomas Penfield Jackson's order to break up the company was an outgrowth of a lengthy and inclusive investigation by the Federal Trade Commission. Next to the verbal and written assaults on Gates, though, the legal one seems almost tepid.

Rob Glaser, a former Microsoft executive who left to run an Internet sound system company, RealAudio, has called his former boss "Darwinian. He doesn't look for win–win situations with others, but for ways to make others lose. Success is defined as flattening the competition, not creating excellence." Thanks to Gates's contentious style, Glaser went on, the Microsoft "atmosphere was like a Machiavellian poker game where you'd hide things even if it would blindside people you were supposed to be working with."

Others like Silicon Valley lawyer Gary Reback maintain that Microsoft uses "its existing monopoly to retard introduction of new technology." The charge is a corollary of another longtime beef especially common among the most cutting-edge high-tech companies and their proponents: that both Gates and his company are evolutionary, not revolutionary. The same complaint could be made about moguls generally, from Cosimo de' Medici to Henry Ford. Just as Cosimo didn't invent banking, so Ford didn't invent the gasoline-powered automobiles; rather, their fortunes came from doing the job better. But in the digital, everything-must-be-new era the charge has gathered resonance.

Gates's immediate rivals seem to take almost demonic glee in attacking the man, his products, and his company. Borland CEO Philippe Kahn once compared Microsoft to Germany under Adolph Hitler; another time, he likened Microsoft's Windows system to AIDS. Lotus founder Mitch Kapor looked around the landscape of the software industry and declared that Microsoft's dominance had left it "the kingdom of the dead." Oracle CEO Larry Ellison is probably the most antagonistic of Gates's many industry competitors. As the Justice Department was moving against Microsoft, Ellison told a May 1998 Harvard computer conference that the company's business practices were "patently illegal . . . more blatant than anything [John D.] Rockefeller ever did" and he accused Gates of "lying" about Microsoft's record of innovation. For good measure, Oracle also hired a Washington detective agency, Investigative Group International, to dig up dirt on its rival, literally going through Microsoft's trash.

In cyberspace, things only get worse. Half a year into the new millennium, you could use a Microsoft operating system and Microsoft Internet Navigator to find Web sites with names like Boycott Microsoft, Punch Bill Gates, the Microsoft Hate Page, Microsoft Boycott Campaign, IHateBillGates.com, and the Bill Gates Personal Wealth Clock, which tracks Gates's gross worth by the fractional second, based on the 141,159,990 million shares of Microsoft he owned as of 1995, adjusted for splits in 1996, 1998, and 1999. As of Friday, December 15, 2000, at 13:45:47 P.M. Eastern Standard Time, with the Microsoft share price sitting at $48.875, Bill Gates was worth $55.1936 billion, the clock noted, or $199,738 for every living American. In case anyone missed the larger point, the clock also included an old Irish saying directly beneath its calculations: "If you want to know what God thinks about money, just look at the people He gives it to."

～

The real Bill Gates is probably best described by a quote attributed to a competitor in the software business who also described himself as a friend of the Microsoft cofounder. Gates, this person said, is "one part Albert Einstein, one part John McEnroe, and one part General Patton"—one part, that is, scientific genius, one part the temperamental genius cum bad boy, and one part tactical genius. For good measure, this person might also have thrown in Thomas Edison, another genius but also an ultra-successful entrepreneur who knew how to turn technological innovation into sales.

Born to wealthy parents in Seattle—where his father was a prominent attorney and his mother a childhood friend of Meg Greenfield, the longtime editorial-page editor of the *Washington Post*—Gates attended the fashionable and academically rigorous Lakeside School. It was there that he and his friend Paul Allen first discovered computing, on a fossilized school terminal bought with the proceeds from a Mothers' Club cookie sale. By 1968, the two eighth graders had learned the BASIC computer language and produced their first programs. Soon, they were spending evenings debugging a computer for a Seattle company. By tenth grade, Gates was writing a program that handled class scheduling for Lakeside. About the same time, he, Paul Allen, and a third friend, Kent Evans, secured jobs writing a payroll system for a local firm and analyzing and graphing traffic data for the City of Seattle. (Evans, probably Gates's best friend from those days, was killed in a mountain climbing accident before the three of them had left high school.)

After graduating from Lakeside in 1973, Gates moved on to Harvard, while Allen went to work for Honeywell. Two years later, in January 1975, came the event enshrined in Microsoft mythology as the moment of conception. As the story goes, Allen, who had driven East to be near his computer pal, held up a copy of the new issue of *Popular Electronics* magazine and shouted at Gates, "It's about to begin!" What inspired Allen was a cover mockup of the MITS (for Micro Instrumentation and Telemetry Systems) Altair 8800, a kit computer that despite its primitive and often unworkable nature was to be the first personal computer. Gates and Allen immediately set out to write a BASIC language for the Altair, and on February 1 of that year, they sold it to MITS, their first customer. Thus it was that Bill Gates became Harvard's most famous dropout— he and Allen set up shop in Albuquerque, New Mexico, where MITS was headquartered—and Microsoft was launched. The conception turned into a very quick birth.

Micro-soft, as it was first spelled, ended 1975 with three employees and $16,005 in revenues, but Gates and Allen were well on their way to settling a fundamental question that was to make all the difference in the company's success: what part of the computing business were they going to be in. Allen, who would leave the company in the early 1980s after a bout with Hodgkin's disease and go on to become a major venture capitalist as well as a sports team owner and the founder of a rock-and-roll museum, had favored a combination of software and hardware. Hardware, after all, was the business that nearly all the computing giants of the time were pursuing. Gates wanted to do software only, and luckily for Microsoft's eventual shareholders, he prevailed.

"When you have the microprocessor doubling in power every two years, in a sense you can think of computer power as almost free," Gates told a *Playboy* interviewer who asked about the rift. "So you ask, Why be in the business of making something that's almost free? What is the scarce resource? What is it that limits being able to get value out of that infinite

237

computing power? Software. Another way to look at it is that I just understood a lot more about software than I did about hardware, so I was sticking to what I knew well—and that turned out to be something important."

By 1980, Microsoft had shed the hyphen, moved to Washington state, and was a 40-person company earning about $7.5 million in revenues. The company would end 1981 with three times as many employees and more than double the revenue. What happened in between was IBM. The computer giant had come calling with a request: Would Microsoft be willing to develop languages and an operating system for IBM's first personal computer? On August 12, 1981, IBM introduced with great fanfare its Personal Computer. Far less noticed at the time was the 16-bit brain inside the PC—Microsoft's Disk Operating System, or MS-DOS, for short—or the fact that Gates had pressured the industry behemoth into giving Microsoft sole rights to license MS-DOS. For Bill Gates and Microsoft, the train had left the station.

"We wanted to make sure only we could license it," Gates has said. "We did the deal with them at a fairly low price, hoping that would help popularize it.... We knew that good IBM products are usually cloned, so it didn't take a rocket scientist to figure out that eventually we could license DOS to others. We knew that if we were ever going to make a lot of money on DOS, it was going to come from the compatible guys, not from IBM."

And make a lot of money, Microsoft certainly would. Given an enormous leg up by IBM's failure to take control of its own operating system, Gates and company by the mid-1980s had won the personal-computer operating systems war and were turning their attention toward domination of what's known as the "office suite": the combination of word processing, spreadsheet, and presentation. Each new conquest further engrained MS-DOS and, later, its Windows successors as the industry standard. Happily for Microsoft, too, the company made money even when its operating system wasn't sold. Under an agreement that Gates' critics would come to deride as the "computer tax," all manufacturers of IBM personal computer clones had to pay Microsoft a royalty on every computer shipped, whether or not the machine was equipped with MS-DOS.

By the mid-1980s, Microsoft's market dominance was beginning to pay off in a serious fashion. Revenues for 1985 stood at over $140 million, more than nine times what they had been when the company's operating system was first introduced. The next year, on March 13, 1986, the company went public, at $21 a share with the price rising to $28 by the end of the trading day. (Fourteen years later, one of those original shares was worth about $10,000, adjusting for stock splits.) It was, of course, only the beginning.

A second revolution in computing—this one led by Bob Kahn, Vint Cerf, and others—had been underway ever since the 1960s when the Defense Department's Advanced Research Projects Agency had authorized an experiment in networking known as the Arpanet. As the Arpanet evolved into the Internet, the digital interconnection of the world was launched, with all the new economic opportunities that entailed. To make certain that computer users would head into cyberspace using Microsoft products, the company gave away its Internet navigation software, called the MS Internet Explorer. It had the cash reserves to afford the luxury, and the killer competitive instincts to dry up its competitors' bottom lines. To make certain that its navigator would never fly far from its basic operating system and its users would never fly far from home, Microsoft bundled the Internet Explorer with Windows and created, in mid-1995, MSN—the Microsoft Network—as a full-service Internet portal. Within its first three months, MSN had enrolled more than half a million members. Thus what was by far the most popular personal computer operating software became by far the most popular Web exploration software. In time, Microsoft would spread itself all over the Internet and intranets, and into multimedia, on-line magazine publishing, Web TV, and just about anywhere else that a company with a limitless appetite and some $15 billion in annual revenues could take it.

Just as had been the case with Standard Oil almost nine decades earlier, the Justice Department and courts seemed unable to slow Gates's company down, even when the government appeared to have won. In February 1999, StatMarket, an Internet fact gatherer, reported that the Microsoft Internet Explorer was being used by nearly 65 percent of all Net surfers worldwide. By June 2000, after Judge Jackson had ruled against Microsoft in the antitrust case, more than 86 percent of global surfers were using the Internet Explorer—an increase of 32 percent in a scant 16 months that had been highlighted by a nonstop legal assault against the company. What's more, 93 percent of global Net surfers were also using a Microsoft licensed Windows operating system product, StatMarket found.

Bill Gates, who prefers to think of himself as a technologist, not a businessman, had become both one of the world's most admired men and one of its most despised men, as well as its richest citizen.

⁓

John D. Rockefeller was in his early 70s when the breakup of Standard Oil ordered by the Supreme Court helped to triple his fortune in two short years to just under $1 billion. Henry Ford was 45 before he sold his first Model T and in his 60s before he became the world's first billionaire. By age 43, Bill Gates, was a billionaire nearly 80 times over.

In the digital era, the speed at which information travels wasn't the only thing accelerating. So was the speed at which wealth accumulates, products seize their markets, and new ideas turn into the geese that lay golden eggs. Radio needed 20 years to garner 10 million listeners. Television halved that to 10 years. Netscape got to 10 million users in only 28 months, and Hotmail made it in a quarter of the time—a mere 7 months.

One year into the new millennium, 350 million people globally were expected to be using the Internet, according to *Computer Industry Almanac*. By the end of 2005, the wired world-wide population is predicted to hit 765 million people, and as the numbers grow, the digital wealth will spread. At the outset of the twenty-first century, about 43 percent of all Internet users were Americans; by 2005, that figure should drop to 28 percent. Almost overnight, Australia and Finland, the 11 time zones of the former Soviet Union, New Delhi, Madagascar, Rome, and New York City had all become just a log-on away. A web had been created—a literal web: Touch it anywhere and you are in touch with its whole being. And as the Web was spreading exponentially, opportunity was spreading with it. Microsoft, AOL, Macintosh, Lotus, Netscape, Bill Gates, Steve Case, Steve Jobs, Vint Cerf, Bob Kahn, and tens of thousands of others had all played a role in launching an opportunity machine such as the world had never known—one that spread the chance for a better economic life to places that can seem almost unimaginable.

For hundreds of years, the women of the tiny village of Tan Mixay (pronounced *taan meesay*) have lived simply, nearly untouched by the outside world. They spin silk and weave it into intricate designs passed down through generations. Their country, Laos, is one of the least developed nations on the planet—a victim of decades of war and revolution. For most people who live there, "the market" means what it meant to their parents and grandparents and ancestors going back centuries: the town square where local produce is bought and sold. Just as they have been for generations, fishing and farm-ing are the main means for eking a living out of the nation's meager resources. To see how the new interconnected world creates opportunity, though, it's useful to look at three women who have made their global interconnection in this once unlikely place: Me Tha, Vivian Wee, and Nikone Nanong. The odds are against any of them ever becoming a Bill Gates, but the changes they are involved in may be even more pro-found.

Since she was a child, Me Tha has woven silk just as her mother and grandmother did before her, selling and trading among her neighbors in Tan Mixay, but soon her silks will be available on the Internet. No stay-at-home, Vivian Wee trav-els the world, helping businesses in remote countries like Laos learn how to use e-commerce and the World Wide Web so they can compete globally and take advantage of the global appetite for goods. Between the two, half as broker, half as facilitator, stands Nikone Nanong. Born into a typical Lao family where girls are expected to learn weaving as part of their marriage skills, Nikone like Godric and legions of entrepreneurs before her aspired to more. In 1992, with $1,000 in start-up capital and six looms, she launched Nikone's Handcraft Center in Laos' capital, Vientiane. By the start of the new century, those six looms had grown into a business that employs 150 women from all over Laos. Some of them work in the handcraft cen-ter; others like Me Tha remain in their own village, where they can care for their children. Where they do the weaving is immaterial because all the women are linked to the same global marketplace through Nikone's website, where she sells all her silks. That marketplace expands constantly as each new link to the Internet is made, and as the marketplace expands, the potential for profit expands exponentially with it. ("The value of a network goes up as the square of the users," as Bob Metcalf, founder of the Ethernet, has put it.)

Nikone's Internet site (www.aworldforall.com) is operated by A World for All, a nonprofit foundation dedicated to improving community life in impoverished areas. The site includes artisans from Cambodia, Thailand, and Vietnam, as well as Nikone's Lao weavers. The goods for sale—mostly textiles—range from simple pillowcases to more ornate throws. Most items sell for about $50; just a few climb to over $200. The site itself is absent the bells and whistles common to so many cyber-trading posts. In a global Internet economy measurable in the trillions of dollars, the trade generated at aworldforall.com is not even a drop in the bucket, but it's a vital drop all the same. Through the site, craftspeople working in some of the world's most forlorn economies can compete with other weavers and textile entrepreneurs in every corner of the planet. And in a nation like Laos where yearly income in 1999 averaged less than $1,300 a person, it takes only a relatively few e-business sales to make an enormous difference in the standard of living for the craftspeople and the families and communities they help support.

"How many people in the world are going to Laos?" Vivian Wee asks. "How many people are going to be sitting next to a village weaver to see how she weaves? The number who do that is so small compared to the number who can click on her website and visit Nikone."

"We are so far away," Nikone adds. "I had never dreamed to be on the Internet." Now that she is, though, global exposure gives her one more advantage, she says: "I can convince my staff, 'You must work hard and you must be more responsible for your thing, because now it's on the Web.'"

The Netherlands grew rich in the sixteenth and seventeenth centuries as a trading center where rare goods brought out of North Africa, the Levant, and further East at great cost could begin to make their way to the marketplaces of Europe. Godric grew rich a half a millennium earlier by doing much the same at far greater risk. Faith in the power of business is inextinguishable. But today, the Internet accomplishes all that Godric and the Dutch East India traders did in the blink of an eye. Goods from all over the globe are available to shoppers all over the globe, twenty-four hours a day and via every sort of barter exchange: meet a price, name a price, bid a price, bid a swap.

The Medicis grew rich through financial exchange. If you wanted a substantial loan in fifteenth century Europe—one to raise an army or support a pope—you were wise to get yourself to Florence or to one of Medicis' partner banks elsewhere on the continent. For smaller concerns or more immediate needs, there were the *banchi di pegni*—the pawnbrokers—and the *banchi in mercado,* the forerunners of today's neighborhood banks. Whichever one you dealt with and wherever, the exchange was sure to be in currency backed by precious metals: A Florentine florin consisted of 3.52 grams of 24-karat gold, exactly and always.

Today, through the Internet, stocks, bonds, mortgages, and mutual funds are all bought and sold on line, and currency trade has become the largest market in the world. Money crisscrosses the globe at the click of a mouse, and nothing real underlies it. Only a hundred years ago, a dollar bill still had to be backed up with a dollar's worth of gold or silver. Today, money is essentially electronic blips racing through electric wires, bouncing off satellites: No currency anywhere in the world is backed by anything more than sheer faith.

Matthew Boulton and James Watt dramatically reduced the size of the steam engine and gave it greatly increased utility, but they didn't dematerialize it. To get the advantage of a Boulton and Watt engine, you still had to have one installed and on location. Henry Ford and John D. Rockefeller both needed vast physical infrastructures to support their fortune making. Now the Internet provides both the power source and the bulk of the infrastructure for many businesses like Nikone's

Handcraft Center—at a fraction of the cost. The Net is not only an information highway; it's also what the influential CEO of EDventure Holdings Inc., Esther Dyson, has called "an information bicycle"—an infrastructure built for personal freedom, one that allows entrepreneurs to do what they want to do, in whatever fashion makes sense, whether it's e-trading Hummel figurines or selling silk like your parents and parents' parents have always made but to infinitely bigger and better markets.

Throughout the last millennium, it was control that created fortunes: control over the oceans or the railroads, the highways or the airwaves. At the start of the new millennium, it's still control—this time over cyberspace, the new wealth machine. Some things never change, but here's the great difference: This road to riches is open to everyone.

◈ Acknowledgments ◈

HANKING EVERYONE RESPONSIBLE FOR A DOCUMEN-
tary or a book alone can run to many pages.
Thanking everyone who has helped with a book
born from a documentary entails a double debt
that will be inadequately paid in this brief space.

First, profound thanks to David Grubin Productions, which created the magnificent documentary that is the basis of this book along with producers Ed Gray and Nick Davis, assisted by Amanda Pollak, Annie Wong, and Alex Dionne. I'm especially grateful to David Grubin, who not only created the idea but furnished me with a terrific script from which to work, and to Lesley Norman for all her help.

Special gratitude is owed to CNBC, which not only aired "Money and Power" but helped in ways big and small to shape my thinking and words, especially Bill Bolster and Bruno Cohen, who helped create the concept and make it happen; Charles MacLachlan and Andrew Darrow for all their support for the documentary and involvement in all aspects of the creation of this book; and Karin Annus for her comments on the manuscript.

Credit goes also to all those who took time from busy schedules to impart their knowledge, wisdom, and insight in front of the cameras and subsequently to these pages: Frederick Allen, Stephen Ambrose, Jim Andrews, David Bain, Alan Brinkley, Edward Chancellor, Ron Chernow, Esther Dyson, Neal Gabler, John Steele Gordon, Henry Grunwald, Joel Kaye, Dale Kent, Maury Klein, David Landes, Joe Lennox, David Lewis, Nikone Nanong, Jean Strouse, Jennifer Tann, Steven Watts, Jack Weatherford, and Vivian Wee.

Thanks as well to those who helped in more anonymous ways to broaden my vision, sharpen my understanding, and

247

resolve the often microscopic points that can be the biggest stumbling blocks in a project of this scope. Among the many: Paul Chernoff, Greg DeVito, Benjamin Lamberton, my nephew Tom Means, and my wife Candy, always the most reliable source. I'm grateful to *Washingtonian* magazine for the use of its research facilities.

Last, but certainly not least, thanks to my dedicated and passionate editor, Airié Dekidjiev, and her assistant, Jessica Noyes, at John Wiley & Sons; my agent, Raphael Sagalyn, of the Sagalyn Literary Agency; and Claire Huismann at Impressions Book and Journal Services.

Howard Means
Bethesda, Maryland

⚜ Source Notes ⚜

Major sources for *Money and Power* include the following:

1. ST. GODRIC: GOD AND PROFIT

On-air interviews: Joe Lennox, Jack Weatherford

Buechner, Frederick. *Godric*. New York: HarperCollins, 1980.

Coulton, G.G., ed. *Social Life in Britain from the Conquest to the Reformation.* Cambridge: Cambridge University Press, 1918.

Elson, John. "The Millennium of Discovery." *Time* (October 15, 1992): 16 ff.

Kaye, Joel. *Economy and Nature in the Fourteenth Century.* Cambridge: Cambridge University Press, 1998.

McDonald, John. "Domesday Economy." *National Institute Economic Review* (April 1, 2000): 105 ff.

Pirenne, Henri. *Medieval Cities: The Origins and the Revival of Trade.* Princeton University Press, 1925.

2. COSIMO DE' MEDICI: PUTTING MONEY TO WORK

On-air interviews: John Steele Gordon, Joel Kaye, Dale Kent, Jack Weatherford

Brucker, Gene. *Renaissance Florence.* Berkeley and Los Angeles: University of California Press, 1969.

Calkins, Hugh. "Can Florence in the Quatrocentro Help Shape Tax Policy Today?" *The Tax Lawyer* (Spring 1991): 685 ff.

de Roover, Raymond. *The Rise and Decline of the Medici Bank.* 1999.

Green, Timothy. "From a Pawnshop to Patron of the Arts in Five Centuries." *Smithsonian* (July 1991): 58 ff.

Hale, J.R. *Florence and the Medici.* Thames and Hudson, 1977.

Hibbert, Christopher. *The House of Medici: Its Rise and Fall.* Morrow, Quill, 1974.

Jardine, Lisa. *Worldly Goods.* Bantam Doubleday Dell, 1996.

Kent, Dale. *The Rise of the Medici.* Oxford: Oxford University Press, 1978.

Le Goff, Jacques. *Your Money or Your Life: Economy and Religion in the Middle Ages.* Cambridge: MIT Press, 1990.

Weatherford, J. McIver. *The History of Money.* New York: Crown, 1997.

3. PHILIP II: WEALTH WITHOUT WISDOM

On-air interviews: John Steele Gordon, David Landes

Dash, Mike. *Tulipmania*. Crown Publishers, 1999.

Kamen, Henry. *Philip of Spain*. New Haven, CT: Yale University Press, 1997.

Landes, David S. *The Wealth and Poverty of Nations*. New York: W.W. Norton, 1998.

Martin, Colin, and Geoffrey Parker. *The Spanish Armada*. New York: W.W. Norton, 1992.

Perez-Diaz, Victor. "State and Public Sphere in Spain During the Ancient Regime." *Daedalus* (June 22, 1998): 251 ff.

Rocca, Francis X. "Philip of Spain." *Atlantic Monthly* (August 1997): 85 ff.

4. TULIPMANIA: SHARING THE GREED

On-air interviews: Edward Chancellor, John Steele Gordon, David Landes

Chancellor, Edward. *Devil Take the Hindmost*. New York: Farrar, Straus and Giroux, 1999.

Dash, Mike. *Tulipmania*, Crown Publishers, 1999.

Garber, Peter. "Who Put the Mania in Tulipmania?" *The Journal of Portfolio Management* (Fall 1989): 53 ff.

Gordon, John Steele. *The Great Game*. New York: Simon & Schuster, 1999.

Landes, David S. *The Wealth and Poverty of Nations*. New York: W.W. Norton, 1998.

Rigby, Rhymer. "The True Story of Flower Power." *Management Today* (June 1997): 94 ff.

Schama, Simon. *The Embarrassment of Riches*. Zane, 1987.

**5. JAMES WATT AND MATTHEW BOULTON:
TURNING EVOLUTION INTO REVOLUTION**

On-air interviews: Jim Andrews, John Steele Gordon, David Landes, Jennifer Tann

Arnot, Chris. "The Master Bauble-Maker." *The Guardian* (October 14, 1995): T66.

Crowther, J.G. *Scientists of the Industrial Revolution*.

Dickinson, H.W. *Matthew Boulton*. Cambridge: Cambridge University Press, 1936.

Landes, David S. *The Wealth and Poverty of Nations*. New York: W.W. Norton, 1998.

Lord, John. *Capital and Steam Power*. 1923.

Powell, John. "The Birmingham Coiners, 1770–1816." *History Today* (July 1993): 49 ff.

Rocco, Fiametta. "Keeping the Flame." *Institutional Investor* (December 1988): 31 ff.

Tann, Jennifer. *The Selected Papers of Boulton and Watt* (Vol. 1). Cambridge: MIT Press, 1981.

Webb, Robert N. *James Watt: Inventor of a Steam Engine.* Franklin Watts, 1970.

6. THE TRANSCONTINENTAL RAILROAD:
ROGUES AND VISIONARIES

On-air interviews: Stephen Ambrose, David Bain, Maury Klein

Ambrose, Stephen. *Nothing Like It in the World.* New York: Simon & Schuster, 2000.

Bain, David. *Empire Express.* New York: Viking Penguin, 1999.

———. Interview. "Booknotes." C-Span by Brian Lamb, March 5, 2000.

Klein, Maury. *Union Pacific.* New York: Doubleday, 1987.

Lewis, Oscar. *The Big Four.* New York: Alfred A. Knopf, 1959.

New York Times. May 11, 1869.

Washington Evening Star. May 10, 1869.

7. J. PIERPONT MORGAN: THE AMERICAN COLOSSUS

On-air interviews: Ron Chernow, John Steele Gordon, Jean Strouse

"The Centennial Exposition." *The Manufacturer and Builder* (July 1876): 148 ff.

Chernow, Ron. *Death of the Banker.* New York: Vintage Books, 1997.

———. *The House of Morgan.* New York: Grove/Atlantic, 1990.

Dos Passos, John. *U.S.A.* New York: Harcourt, Brace and Company, 1930.

New York Times. April 1, 1913.

Strouse, Jean. Interview by Brian Lamb. "Booknotes." C-Span, May 23, 1999.

———. *Morgan.* New York: Random House, 1999.

8. JOHN D. ROCKEFELLER: ORGANIZING THE OCTOPUS

On-air interviews: Ron Chernow, John Steele Gordon

Chernow, Ron. *Titan.* New York: Random House, 1998.

———. Interview by Brian Lamb. "Booknotes." C-Span, June 21, 1998.

Parker, Richard. "Mr. Big." *Los Angeles Times Book Review* (May 31, 1998): 12.

Useem, Jerry. "Entrepreneur of the Century." *Inc.* (May 1999): 158 ff.

9. HENRY FORD:
BUILDING CARS AND THE MARKETS FOR THEM

On-air interviews: David Lewis, Steven Watts

Colbert, David, ed. *Eyewitness to America*. New York: Pantheon Books, 1997.

Foster, Bellamy. "The Fetish of Fordism." *Monthly Review* (March 1988): 14 ff.

Lewis, David. *Management of Non-Governmental Organizations*. New York: Routledge, 2000.

10. ROBERT WOODRUFF: THE BRAND'S THE THING

On-air interviews: Frederick Allen, John Steele Gordon

Allen, Frederick. *Secret Formula*. Collingdale, PA: DIANE Publishing, 1999.

New York Times. March 9, 1985.

Pendergrast, Mark. *For God, Country and Coca-Cola*. New York: Basic Books, 1993.

11. TIME WARNER:
TURNING OPPOSITE CULTURES TO COMMON ADVANTAGE

On-air interviews: Alan Brinkley, Neal Gabler, Henry Grunwald

Brinkley, Alan. "To See and Know Everything." *Time* (March 9, 1998): 90.

Gabler, Neal. "Behind the Scenes at Warner Brothers." *Los Angeles Times Magazine* (July 31, 1988): 17 ff.

———. *An Empire of Their Own*. New York: Crown, 1988.

———. *Life the Movie*. New York: Alfred A. Knopf, 1998.

Hift, Fred. "Hollywood Be Thy Name." *Video Age International* (May 1994): 12 ff.

Sperling, Cass Warner and Cork Milner. *Hollywood Be Thy Name*. Lexington, KY: The University Press of Kentucky, 1998.

12. BILL GATES AND CYBERSPACE:
THE DEMATERIALIZED FUTURE

On-air interviews: Esther Dyson, John Steele Gordon, Nikone Nanong, Jean Strouse, Jack Weatherford, Vivian Wee

Dyson, Esther. *Release 2.1*. New York: Broadway Books, 1997.

Gates, Bill. "Playboy Interview," Interview by David Rensin, *Playboy* (July 1994): 55 ff.

SOURCE NOTES

————. *The Road Ahead.* New York: Viking Penguin, 1995.
Isaacson, Walter. "In Search of the Real Bill Gates." *Time* (January 13, 1997): 44 ff.
"Timelines." Microsoft Museum. www.microsoft.com.

Major general sources for *Money and Power* include the following:

American National Biography. New York: Oxford University Press, 1999.
Dictionary of Scientific Biography. New York: Charles Scribner's Sons, 1970.
Encyclopedia Britannica. Chicago: Encyclopedia Britannica, Inc., 1969.
Encyclopedia of the Middle Ages. New York: Facts on File, 1995.
Encyclopedia of the Renaissance. New York: Charles Scribner's Sons, 1999.
Historical Abstracts of the United States. Washington, D.C.: U.S. Department of Commerce, Bureau of the Census, 1975.
Smith, George David and Frederick Dalzell, eds. *Wisdom from the Robber Barons.* Cambridge, MA: Perseus Publishing, 2000.

❧ Photo Credits ❧

July: Making Hay. Da Costa Hours
Source: Bening, Simon (1483–1561), Bruges, c. 1515. M.399, f.8v. Pierpont
  Morgan Library/Art Resource New York.

Dante Holding the Divine Comedy (with purgatory to the left, and the Cathedral
  of Florence to the right)
Source: Alinari/Art Resource New York.

El Greco: *View of Toledo*
Source: The Metropolitan Museum of Art. Bequest of Mrs. H.O. Havemeyer,
  1929, The H.O. Havemeyer Collection.

Flower Bouquet with Tulips, oil on Mahogany
Source: Art Resource New York.

Photo of Watt's steam engine
Reproduced from the Collections of the Library of Congress. US262 29906
  201537.

"10 Miles of Train Track, Laid in One Day"
Source: Used by permission, Utah State Historical Society, all rights reserved.
  Photo no. 522.

Rush on an East Side Bank (crowd gathered outside of a bank, 1907)
Source: Reproduced from the Collections of the Library of Congress.

Portrait of John D. Rockefeller
Source: The Western Reserve Historical Society, 10825 East Boulevard, Cleveland, Ohio 44106.

Model T Ford photo
Source: Library of Congress. LC-USZ62-34885.

Robert Woodruff in front of a Coca-Cola billboard
Source: Coca-Cola.

Poster for Warner Bros. film

Bill Gates with schoolchildren
Source: AP Worldwide.

255

♣ Index ♣

257

Index

Money
  changers, 33
  introduction of modern banking
    system, 31
Mongol dynasty, 30
Monks of Farne, 23
Monopolies
  Casa de Contratacion (House of
    Trade), 49
  East India Trade Company, 68
  Microsoft, 234
  tulips, 73
Monti di pieta (pity for the needy), 34
Morgan: American Financier (Jean
    Strouse), 132
Morgan Bank, 139
Morgan, J. Pierpoint, 127–144
  assets, 143
  crisis management, 140
  death of, 130, 142
  financing of railroads, 135–136
  raising capital to purchase railroads,
    135–136
  rescue of financial disasters,
    138–140
  youth of, 133
Morgan, Junius Spencer (J.S.), 134, 137
Moriscos (Spanish-born Muslims), 58
Mormons, 120
Motion Pictures Patent Company, 211
Motley, John Lothrop, 51
Movies, 208
  introduction of sound in, 212
  See also Time Warner
MS-DOS (Microsoft Disk Operating
    System), 230
MSN (Microsoft Network), 239
Murdoch, William, 93, 98, 101
Museum of Modern Art, 153
Muslim religion, during the Spanish
    Inquisition, 57

My Four Years in Germany (James W.
    Gerard), 211
My Life & Work (Henry Ford), 172

National Socialist Party (Germany), 182
NBC (National Broadcast Company),
    207
Nelson, Lord, 99
Net. *See* Internet
Netherlands, 18, 48
  Amsterdam, 72
  Coca-Cola, 200
  trade policies of, 68
  wars (Philip II), 58
Netscape, 241
New Castle, Pennsylvania, 210
Newcomen, Thomas, 88
New Meeting Church, 92
Newspapers
  Chicago Tribune, 174
  New York Sun, 122
  New York Times, 110, 123
  Washington *Evening Star*, 108–111
  Washington Post, 236
  Yale Daily News, 219
New World
  arrival of Christopher Columbus, 47
  as a diminishing asset, 59
  gold and silver as currency for
    Spanish wars, 57–58
  Philip II, King. *See* Philip II, King
  Spanish settlers, 59
New York City, preservation of credit,
    141
New York Stock Exchange, 130, 137
New York Sun, 122
New York Times, 110, 123
New York University, 160
Nikone's Handcraft Center, 242
Nineteen, Nineteen (John Dos Passos), 133
Northern Pacific Railroad, 127, 136

267